GHOSTHUNTING
OHIO

ON THE ROAD AGAIN

AMERICA'S
HAUNTED ROAD TRIP

Titles in the *America's Haunted Road Trip* Series:

Ghosthunting Colorado
Ghosthunting Florida
Ghosthunting Kentucky
Ghosthunting Illinois
Ghosthunting Maryland
Ghosthunting Michigan
Ghosthunting New Jersey
Ghosthunting New York City
Ghosthunting North Carolina
Ghosthunting Ohio
Ghosthunting Ohio: On the Road Again
Ghosthunting Oregon
Ghosthunting Pennsylvania
Ghosthunting San Antonio, Austin, and Texas Hill Country
Ghosthunting Southern California
Ghosthunting Southern New England
Ghosthunting Texas
Ghosthunting Virginia

Chicago Haunted Handbook
Cincinnati Haunted Handbook
Nashville Haunted Handbook
Haunted Hoosier Trails
More Haunted Hoosier Trails
Spirits of New Orleans
Spooked in Seattle
Twin Cities Haunted Handbook

GHOSTHUNTING
OHIO
ON THE ROAD AGAIN

JOHN B. KACHUBA

CLERISY PRESS

Ghosthunting Ohio: On the Road Again

For further information, contact the publisher at:

Clerisy Press
An imprint of AdventureKEEN
306 Greenup Street
Covington, KY 41011
www.clerisypress.com

Library of Congress Cataloging-in-Publication Data
Kachuba, John B.
    Ghosthunting Ohio : on the road again / by John Kachuba. — 1st ed.
        p. cm. — (America's haunted road trip)
    ISBN-13: 978-1-57860-491-3 (pbk.)
    ISBN-10: 1-57860-491-5 (pbk.)
    ISBN 978-1-57860-492-0 (ebook)
    ISBN 978-1-57860-595-8 (hardcover)
    1. Haunted places—Ohio. 2. Ghosts—Ohio. I. Title. II. Series.

    BF1472.U6K34 2011
    133.109771—dc23
                                        2011022285

Distributed by Publishers Group West

First edition, first printing

Editor: Andy Sloan
Cover design: Scott McGrew
Cover and interior photos provided by the author unless otherwise noted

For Bree and Corrine

Table of Contents

Introduction

HEY, GHOSTHUNTER, *when are you going to tell us about more haunted places in Ohio?* If I had a nickel for every time someone asked me that question, I would be a rich man today. Almost immediately after *Ghosthunting Ohio* was published in 2004, people began asking me why I didn't include this haunted place or that one in the book. It seemed that every time I was a guest on some paranormal radio show, or speaking at a library or university, I would be asked that question. Who knew that there were so many haunted locations in Ohio? I did eventually listen to what my fans and readers were telling me, and this is the result: *Ghosthunting Ohio: On the Road Again.*

As all the books in the America's Haunted Road Trip series, this book is a paranormal travel guide, designed to provide not only a great ghost story about each location but also practical information for those of you who would like to do a little ghost-hunting of your own. Each place is open to the public, and specific details about location, hours of operation, phone numbers and website addresses, etc., are provided in the Resources section in the back of the book.

Southwest

Cincinnati
Cincinnati Observatory

Loveland
Chateau Laroche

Milford
Promont House Museum

New Richmond
Ross Gowdy House

New Vienna
Snow Hill Country Club

3

CHAPTER 1

Chateau Laroche
LOVELAND

I COULDN'T BELIEVE MY EYES. There, on a grassy sward beside the river, two knights in armor and colorful livery were engaged in furious combat, slashing away at each other with swords that looked as if they were made of rattan, while a bevy of ladies in long gowns and wimples stood beneath the trees watching them in fear and admiration. To the right, a mighty Norman castle rose up on the hillside overlooking the river, flags flying from its crenellated towers: the redoubtable Chateau Laroche. I felt as though I had wandered into a chapter from *Ivanhoe*, but in fact I was in Loveland, Ohio, only a few minutes away from downtown Cincinnati.

I lived in Loveland for several years and had the occasion many times to visit Chateau Laroche—nicknamed the Loveland Castle—with my children, friends, and out-of-town visitors. While medieval reenactors were not always on hand, you could depend upon someone from the Knights of the Golden Trail, the present owners and curators of the castle, to show you around and to answer questions about this incredible architectural wonder, the dream-child and life's work of one man, "Sir" Harry Andrews.

You could also rely on the Knights to tell you about the several ghosts that sought refuge in the castle's musty stone walls. The ghosts are an integral and romantic part of the history of the castle that all began in 1929 when Sir Harry bought the property on the banks of the Little Miami River and single-handedly began to construct his one-quarter-scale Norman castle.

What would prompt a man to devote himself to such an arduous task?

Harry Andrews was a fascinating man. Born in 1890, he was a graduate of Colgate University, reportedly spoke seven languages, and had an amazing IQ of 189. He enlisted in the U.S. Army during World War I, serving as a medic, even though he was a conscientious objector. He did not object to warfare itself, but to the weapons of modern warfare that could indiscriminately kill large numbers of people from a distance; Harry preferred the old chivalric way of killing a man in eye-to-eye, hand-to-hand combat. During the war, he contracted spinal meningitis and was declared dead. By the time he was declared "undead" six months later, his fiancée back home had married another man.

Rather than return to the United States immediately, Harry roamed throughout Europe studying castles. He also swore off women and over the rest of his life would turn down more than fifty—by his count—marriage proposals from, in his words, "widows and old maids who wanted to live in a castle."

Harry eventually returned to Ohio, where he worked at a local newspaper and conducted Sunday school for boys. He founded the Knights of the Golden Trail for boys and regularly hosted them on his riverside property where they camped, fished, swam, and boated. Deciding that his boys needed a castle, he began hauling rocks up from the river and Chateau Laroche was begun. At first, he worked on the construction whenever he could find the time, but after retiring from the newspaper at the age of sixty-five, he moved into the castle and dedicated all of his time to its completion.

I was fortunate enough to have visited the castle while Sir Harry was still alive and can remember seeing the wiry, white-haired, bespectacled man high up on the castle roof laying bricks. He was still actively working on the castle in 1981, at the age of ninety-one, when his pants accidentally caught fire from some work he was doing on the roof. He was severely burned and died sixteen days later from gangrene.

With the exception of some menial odd jobs performed by the young Knights, Sir Harry single-handedly built the castle, laying every brick himself. In addition to river rock, he also made cement bricks, using wax milk cartons as forms. He was a meticulous record-keeper; here is his tally of his labors over the fifty-two years he worked on the castle:

2,600 sacks of concrete

32,000 one-quart milk cartons for brick forms

54,000 five-gallon buckets of dirt

56,000 pails-full of stone

The eccentric lord of the castle received much publicity, and well over one million people have toured the castle. Many of them have seen the ghosts.

Sir Harry began seeing ghosts on the property early on. In his writings, he talked about a ghost he named Casper Poltergeist who he said spent the day resting on a daybed in the castle, getting up at midnight to wander around the castle and play tricks on visitors, such as pounding on the door and ringing the doorbell. Harry wrote, "He will not harm anybody unless you get him angry. Then he will touch you and give you an electric shock, sometimes a hard one."

In addition to the poltergeist, Harry recalled a ghost that looked like "a big Viking dressed in a long, dark cloak, wearing a spiked helmet, and carrying a short, wide sword across his chest." Thankfully, the berserker ghost made his appearance known only a few times before disappearing for good.

Harry also saw a girl in a long dress walking on the water across the river and making herself comfortable on the seats on top of the garage.

But the ghost that was most familiar to Harry lived with him at the castle for sixteen years. According to Harry, the ghost was "shaped like an egg outline, with two big eyes near the smaller end. He was transparent like plastic and grass and weeds could be seen right through him." Harry said that the ghost lived near a willow tree on the property and that he could talk to it, although if anyone else tried to speak to the ghost, it would disappear and Harry would have to coax it to return, something like a skittish pup. Harry wrote that "thousands" of people saw the ghost and that some women would scream and faint when they saw it. The willow tree eventually died, and the ghost must have died with it; he was never seen again.

It's easy to imagine ghosts at the castle, even in broad daylight. The cold brick walls deaden sound, creating an interior that is eerily silent. I could feel my ears ringing in the silence. The replica pieces of armor that stand sentinel in the halls and rooms seemed as though they were watching me, and I could not help but wonder if they harbored the spirits of long-gone knights. The narrow, twisting tower staircase to the upper level was designed deliberately in that manner as a defensive measure; an attacking archer could not shoot up the stairs at defenders, and the narrow passage effectively blocked invaders from advancing in groups. But for me, visiting the castle alone, there was the foreboding sense of not knowing what might be standing on the next step to greet me as I ascended.

The little bedroom off the ballroom on the second floor in which Sir Harry lived is much as he left it, with a small bed and cookstove. Standing in the doorway, peering into the tiny room, I could almost see Harry once again. To complete the shadowy tour, below the castle is a delightful little dungeon, complete with a grinning skeleton behind a barred door.

"Sir" Joe has been a fixture at Chateau Laroche for a long time. As a boy, he was one of Harry's Knights, and he continues to safeguard Harry's legacy to this day. I had spoken with him on a few visits to the castle and had once interviewed him at length for a newspaper article I wrote about the castle. Thin and sinewy, with a voice that reminded me of *King of the Hill*'s Dale Gribble, Sir Joe loved to tell stories about the castle, especially ghost stories.

He told me that Boy Scouts on overnight visits to the castle often encountered ghostly activity.

"Such as?" I asked.

"They take their shoes off to go to sleep and when they wake up in the morning they may find their shoes all tied together," Joe said.

"Wow."

"Or the chessmen on this chessboard might be moved in different positions from where they were left the night before."

I noted the chessboard and playing pieces set up on a small table; they seemed ordinary enough.

As Sir Joe told me these stories, his expression was more bemused than mystified and I wondered if, just perhaps, the ghostly pranks played upon the Scouts might not have some human agency behind them.

But Joe had some stories of his own to relate. One day, Joe and another Knight, "Sir" Tim, were relaxing in the castle after a long day of work there. Suddenly, the door of the bathroom off the ballroom upstairs slammed shut. The men knew that they were alone at the castle, so they raced upstairs to see who had broken into the building. There was no one there. They went back downstairs, but two more times the door slammed shut by itself.

Sir Joe thought that someone—maybe Sir Harry?—was trying to send them a message, but Sir Tim was skeptical. The next morning, Joe checked the bathroom once more and, finding nothing amiss, went outside to check the plumbing. He found that the lines running to the septic tank were about to overflow, which would have created quite a mess in the castle gardens. Thanks to the warning message from the friendly ghost the night before, the Knights were able to correct the problem in time to avert a disaster.

Despite Sir Harry's aversion to women, the present-day Knights of the Golden Trail have included Ladies among their membership. One such Lady, Donna Jean, experienced a ghost encounter during a Boy Scout overnight. Donna Jean was supervising the event one night in 1989 and, while the Scouts were sitting around a campfire by the river, she made a perimeter check of the grounds. After finding everything secure, she sat down outside to enjoy the warm May night.

She noticed a figure on the road coming up toward the gardens. She described it as "transparent, whitish in color, and very flowing, like a woman with shoulder-length hair and a long billowy gown." The figure approached the garden near where Lady Donna Jean was sitting and then simply disappeared.

She recalled a story that Harry had told the Knights that might explain the ghostly woman. According to Harry, a man and his wife had built a cabin, attached to a cave downriver from the castle, where they made moonshine. One day, while Harry and some young Knights were working at the castle, they heard a loud explosion and ran down to the cabin. It had been destroyed completely in the blast, and in the wreckage they found the dead body of the woman beneath a whiskey barrel.

Since Lady Donna first saw the ghost, she has been seen many times by both Knights and visitors to the castle.

Lady Christie tells of sitting in the castle one night, facing toward Sir Harry's bedroom and the spiral staircase. A Knight was also there, but was taking a shower; they were the only people in the castle. Lady Christie noticed some movement near the staircase. A huge shadow the size of a human was slowly coming up the stairs. She was frightened and called out to Sir Ron, the Knight in the shower. The shadow continued toward the top of the staircase. Lady Christie screamed and ran to the bathroom, pounding on the door to get the wet Knight's attention. By this time, the shadow had reached the top of the stairs and was standing in the archway of the room. Sir Ron emerged from the bathroom and also felt the presence of something paranormal, although the shadow had suddenly disappeared. The Knight and the Lady quickly retreated from the castle.

Chateau Laroche remains a work in progress as the Knights of the Golden Trail maintain not only the physical grounds but the spirit of Sir Harry Andrews as well. Make a trip to this enchanting castle and see if you can find some spirits of your own.

Spotlight On: Spiritual H.O.P.E.

Based in Cincinnati, Spiritual Historians of Paranormal Evidence Society (Spiritual H.O.P.E.) is the only ghosthunter group I know that boasts a canine member; Kodi (short for Kodiak) is a nine-year-old schipperke owned by the group's director of operations, Crystal Ayers. The group's founder, DaShane Watkins, says that Kodi is sensitive to paranormal activity in haunted locations, and the pooch is put to work on most investigation, carrying some of the group's batteries, lights, and EMF meters. In addition to the Cincinnati members, the society now has 200 remote team members located in several chapters.

Spiritual H.O.P.E. Society hosts public investigations called "Ghosts in the Museums" at Glendower Mansion and the Warren County Historical Society Museum, both in Lebanon, Ohio, as well as Hillforest Mansion in Aurora, Indiana. The group donates half of the proceeds from its investigations to the museums to help keep their doors open. In recognition of this work, Watkins has been awarded a Certificate of Appreciation from the Ohio Historical Society for his contributions and for teaching the public about history in an interesting manner. The group was also the first to investigate the haunted Cincinnati Observatory (see the chapter about the observatory in this book).

In addition to conducting investigations, DaShane is a filmmaker and, with Crystal Ayers, cohosts a podcast called "Widespread Paranormal."

DaShane's favorite haunt is the James Rupert house in Hamilton, Ohio. One Easter in the 1970s, Rupert used three different guns to shoot to death eleven members of his family; oddly, no one else heard a single shot. DaShane talks about an investigation he and Crystal conducted at the house:

"I had never been actually touched by something paranormal until that night walking up to the back porch. Crystal and I were walking

Spotlight On: Spiritual H.O.P.E.
(continued)

around the side of the house, and as we headed to the back porch, I was poked in the chest by an unseen force. It felt like the end of a broomstick being poked into my chest very hard. As I jumped back, I turned on the flashlight to see if maybe there was a stray branch poking out from the vines that had grown up the lattice that covered the whole back porch. I thought for sure that I would find a branch that had been freshly cut and was sticking out, but after careful examination, I found nothing to offer an explanation. No branches, sticks, or twigs poking out from the lattice. Nothing. So now my senses were on high alert. Heart pounding, adrenaline pumping. What poked me? Suddenly, in the midst of this, I saw two images flash in my head, a little boy and a girl on the back porch. The flash was in black and white except for the little girl's pink bow on her hat. Then it went away. After doing research on the murders, I found out that the girl was the only one that got close to getting away. She made it as far as the back porch with her brother close behind her before they were shot by the madman."

DaShane reports that, at the same time, Crystal asked the ghost to make the EMF meter she held in her hand record higher readings. It did and Crystal felt something slap the back of her hand, as if to knock the meter out of her grasp. Later, the two discovered that they had recorded two EVPs at that time, a man's voice saying, *I'm doing it* and a growling voice that said, *Get out of here.* Crystal also received mental images from the porch; DaShane notes that neither of them are psychics.

For more information about Spiritual H.O.P.E. Society, go to the group's website at **spiritualhopesociety.com.**

What's in a Name?
Spooky Hollow Road, Indian Hill

The Village of Indian Hill is a Cincinnati-area bedroom community with sprawling mansions and picturesque bridle trails nestled among rolling hills and leafy woods. It's the home of the area's wealthiest movers and shakers and celebrities, such as rocker Peter Frampton.

But Indian Hill may also be home to ghosts. How else can we explain the road named Spooky Hollow Road? An unlighted two-lane road that twists and turns downhill, Spooky Hollow Road is indeed spooky, if you drive it too fast or under the influence of spirits from a bottle.

I checked with the Indian Hill Historical Society to see how the road received its name. In the eighteenth century a man named Eli Dusky operated a sugar camp in the area where he made maple sugar. The story goes that one night, after perhaps imbibing some of the aforementioned spirits, Eli decided to check on his sugar vats and walked through the dark woods to the camp, located in a hollow. When he got there, he saw "hobgoblins" dancing round the vats. Scared out of his wits, Eli ran back to town, raving about the spirits in the hollow. Of course, no one believed him.

No one knows whether or not poor Eli ever returned to his sugar camp, but his story became notorious enough for the road to be named after his adventure.

And no one knows if the hobgoblins continue to dance in Spooky Hollow.

CHAPTER 2

Cincinnati Observatory
CINCINNATI

ONE OF THE PLACES YOU WOULD LEAST EXPECT
to find a ghost would be an astronomical observatory. That was
why I was so surprised when I received an e-mail message from
John Ventre, historian at the Cincinnati Observatory, America's
oldest public observatory.

John explained to me that he had heard me on *Coast-to-
Coast AM with George Noory*, a popular late-night radio show,
and wondered if I would like to visit the observatory. Cryptically,
he said there was "something" at the observatory that might be
of interest to me.

I'm not an idiot; I knew what John meant by "something,"
so I contacted my friend DaShane Watkins, founder of a Cin-

cinnati paranormal investigating team called Spiritual H.O.P.E. (Historians of Paranormal Evidence) and asked him if he'd like to come along with me. On a cold February night, my wife, Mary, and I met with DaShane and a few members of his team at the observatory.

We parked our cars in the cul-de-sac of Observatory Place atop Mount Lookout. Lights gleamed inside the main building. Built in 1873, its silver dome stood prominent above the columned porch of the stately Greek Revival building. The smaller Mitchel Building, named for Ormsby MacKnight Mitchel, who founded the observatory in 1843, sat at the right side of the cul-de-sac. Built in 1903, this building houses the observatory's original telescope, a beautiful brass-and-teak instrument built in Bavaria in 1845—and still fully operational today.

Our group entered through the towering door of the main building, where we met John Ventre. A friendly and gregarious man, John gave us a history of the observatory as we stood in the lobby. He told us that the observatory had originally been located on Mount Ida in 1843; former president John Quincy Adams, who was himself an amateur astronomer, laid the cornerstone of the building. The mount was renamed Mount Adams in his honor. As Cincinnati grew and became more industrialized— and as it became a center for the slaughtering of pigs—the air above the city became hazy and polluted, making stargazing nearly impossible. So, the observatory moved to the Mount Lookout location, where the air was clearer.

John said that both telescopes mounted in the buildings still functioned, but that the observatory today served more as an educational museum of astronomy than as a center of astronomical research. Designed to re-create the conditions of an early twentieth-century observatory, the equipment still needs to be operated manually with pulleys, wheels, and gears.

While all that information was helpful, we still waited to

hear the ghost story we knew was coming. But John was still being cagey. "Here's what I'd like to do," he said. "Why don't you all check out the buildings, do what you do, and then meet up back here. Then, I'll tell you what's going on."

DaShane, Robert and Lori Demmon, Crystal Ayers, and I explored the buildings, while John and Mary waited for us in a lecture room. We were not prepared to do an in-depth investigation, but we did have some equipment, mostly cameras and electromagnetic frequency (EMF) meters, to help us collect data. Working in two groups, we detected a slight and unexplainable rise in EMF on the stairs leading to the telescope room in the main building, but little else that indicated any paranormal activity.

But when we returned to the lecture room, the story that John Ventre related to us gave us hope that there might indeed be "something" in the observatory. John asked us what we had found, and we said nothing other than the EMF readings on the stairs. He smiled at that and said that that was where his story took place.

"After a group of visitors had come down from the dome, one woman was shaking. She told me that she was sensitive to spirits and that there was something going on here. That's how she said it, although she could not be any more specific. She said she felt it in the dome and on the stairs coming down."

"Any idea what she could have been feeling?" I asked.

John then told us about a murder that had taken place in front of the main building in 1986. A woman who had been involved in several domestic disputes with her ex-husband followed him to Observatory Place where she shot him three times, leaving him lying on the ground between his motorcycle and a large rock. She got in her car but then got out again and shot him two more times before finally driving away. The man died at the scene, and the neighborhood kids nicknamed the rock

"Blood Rock." The rock was moved from in front of the building to a side lawn, where it stands today.

Had the observatory visitor detected the ghost of the murdered man? DaShane set up an in-depth investigation at the observatory for a few weeks later. Maybe we would find out.

We all came together again on a bitterly cold night in February, minus my wife, who had sense enough to stay home in a nice warm house. The temperature was below twenty degrees, and snow flurries danced in the night sky. This would be a tough investigation since the rooms in which the telescopes were mounted were not heated.

Before we began, we all sat in the lecture room to discuss how we would proceed. DaShane is a young guy and has not been ghosthunting all that long, but I was impressed by his knowledge and thoroughness; he would call the shots for the investigation. He surprised me when he took a photocopied newspaper article out of a folder.

"Got something for you," he said, a satisfied grin upon his face.

I read the brief article from *The New York Times*, dated September 30, 1943: *Cincinnati, Sept. 29 – Dr. Elliot Smith, aged 68, astronomer at the University of Cincinnati, was found hanging from the telescope mounting at the observatory late today. Coroner Frank M. Coppock issued a verdict of suicide.*

"Holy crap!" I said, impressed by DaShane's research. "How did you find this?"

"Good job," John Ventre interjected.

"You knew about this?" I asked John.

"Yes, but I wanted to see if you would find out about it in your investigation."

"Have there been ghost stories connected with the suicide?" I asked.

"No one has ever seen anything," John said, "but there is a

story about a woman who called the observatory at a time when
no one was in the building. She got a garbled man's voice on
the line. She couldn't understand the voice and thought maybe
it was a malfunction in the phone's answering machine. The
problem was that the answering machine had not been turned
on. She happened to be calling on September 29, the anniversary of Smith's suicide."

I looked at DaShane. He just smiled, pleased with himself.

John went on to explain that Smith had some health problems when he received word that his son was missing in action
against the Japanese in the Pacific. That may have been cause
enough for Smith to take his life. Ironically, his son survived
World War II.

Robert, DaShane, and I began our investigation in the main
building while Lori, Crystal, and John Ventre worked in the
Mitchel Building. We walked up the stairs to the domed room
that housed the telescope from which Dr. Smith had hanged
himself. Walking into the circular room was like walking into a
freezer. Our breath condensed in the frigid air.

In the center of the room the huge telescope pointed sky-
ward, easily twenty feet above our heads. Nearby was a tall ladder that looked more like a narrow set of bleachers mounted on
wheels. Astronomers used the ladder to reach the eyepiece of
the telescope. Or to commit suicide.

"Imagine," I said, to DaShane. "He would have climbed up
that ladder, swung a rope around the gearwork on the telescope,
placed the other end around his neck, and simply stepped off."

The three of us stood there for a moment, and that's when
we heard a low growl from somewhere in the room.

"What was that?" Robert asked. "Did you hear that?"

We had our cameras and voice recorders going and DaShane
asked aloud for the growl to repeat itself, but nothing happened.

"We all heard it, right?" I said.

Robert and DaShane said they had. We agreed that it was a human sound, rather than an animal, and that it had definitely come from within the room. At that point, DaShane tried provoking the ghost by speaking aloud in the room, taunting the spirit for its cowardice in committing suicide.

I am not a big fan of provocation, as I believe we cannot understand the thoughts or motives of those who have passed on, and so we should treat them with respect. I had been on other investigations however, in which spirits were provoked, with mixed results, so DaShane wasn't doing anything different from what other investigators have done. In any case, it didn't work.

"What do you say? Should we try the dowsing rods?" I asked.

I use dowsing rods not only to uncover areas of high energy but also as a means of asking ghosts simple "yes/no" questions. I ask them to move the rods for "yes" and to leave them be for "no."

Robert and DaShane filmed me while I held the rods. When DaShane asked if there was a spirit in the room, the rods slowly crossed one over the other—"yes." We tried to determine the identity of the ghost and received a "yes" response when we asked if it was a brother of Dr. Smith. We also received a "yes" answer when we asked if there was more than one spirit present although, oddly, none were identified as Smith.

After a while our team switched places with the other team. We hurried down the sidewalk in the freezing air to the slightly warmer Mitchel Building. In the telescope room, we all heard far-off music, in an old-fashioned style, although it was too indistinct for us to identify the tune. Considering the isolated location of the building and the fact that it was late at night with nearly subzero temperatures outside, we could find no logical explanation for the music. We heard it for a little while, and then it was gone.

In a small circular office in the building we detected a hot spot on the floor that fluctuated between 90 and 100 degrees. We used a remote thermometer that shoots a laser at a given point and measures precisely the temperature at that point. Everywhere in that room, except for the spot on the floor, measured in the low 70s; even the heating vent was only in the 70s.

Intrigued by this hot spot—haunted locations often have *cold* spots—we went down to the basement. There, we found pipes running below the floor of the office upstairs and thought that we had discovered the source of that high heat, but the pipes were only in the 60-degree range.

After several hours we concluded the investigation and packed up our gear. We briefed John Ventre on what we had found and told him we would meet with him again after DaShane and his team reviewed the many hours of audio and visual data they had collected. I did ask John, however, if Dr. Smith had had a brother. John said he did not.

A few weeks later, we met one more time with John for the *reveal*, as some ghosthunters like to call it. Before we started, John told me that he had been wrong when he told me that Dr. Smith did not have a brother; apparently, he had a half brother. Aha, I thought. Was it the spirit of Smith's half-brother that had answered my question that night?

DaShane presented his findings, which were much more extensive than I thought they would be. There were several EVPs (electronic voice phenomena) recorded that night, including more music. A few shadows that remained unidentifiable were captured on video. Plus, we had the positive responses of my dowsing rods, as well as those on the K2 meters used by the other team (the K2 meters light up if spirits answer questions asked of them).

John, who considered himself a skeptic on the subject of ghosts, was impressed. The investigation did not prove conclusively that there was a ghost, or ghosts, in the Cincinnati Observatory, but it certainly provided enough data for one to think it was possible.

It would be wonderful to conduct another investigation there, perhaps this time beneath a full moon.

Spotlight On:
Ascension Paranormal

Founded in 2007 by Michael Perry, the Cincinnati-based Ascension Paranormal group has five team members with an additional ten on call. The group's services include paranormal investigations of any building or place public or private, and blessing and cleansing of any dwelling. Michael says, "We blend the spiritual and scientific together by using prayer and scientific equipment to document and release any entity at said location."

The group's favorite haunt is the Lake Hope area of southeastern Ohio. Michael says, "Lake Hope is close to many haunted places, including Moonville Tunnel, Moonville Cemetery, Hope Furnace, and Athens, Ohio. We go there every year for the history, beauty and, of course, the paranormal."

You can learn more about Ascension Paranormal at **aparanormal.com**.

CHAPTER 3

Ross Gowdy House
NEW RICHMOND

THE BEAUTIFUL TWO-STORY GREEK REVIVAL
HOME known as the Ross Gowdy House was built in New
Richmond in 1853, during the town's heyday as a steamboat-
manufacturing center. Hard by the Ohio River, the brick house
has been ravaged by floods over the years but has survived them
all. The house is named after its first two owners, David Ross, a

mayor of New Richmond, and Thomas Gowdy, who bought the house in 1865 from Roseanna Ross, one of David Ross's relatives. Two other New Richmond mayors have also lived in the house. Now owned by the nonprofit Historic New Richmond, Inc., the house is open to the public as a museum and local historical center. And, of course, it is open to ghosts.

I didn't know anything about the Ross Gowdy House until I met Melinda Smith, founder of Southern Ohio Apparition Researchers (S.O.A.R.), at the Queen City Paracon in Cincinnati, where I was a speaker. I stopped by the S.O.A.R. information booth, where Melinda's knowledge and expertise in ghosthunting so impressed me that when she later invited me to join S.O.A.R. on an investigation of the Ross Gowdy House, I readily accepted.

I arrived early for the investigation at the house. It was a hot, dry July evening, and what Melinda and her team had not planned for was the band concert in the park right next door to the house. Now I like John Philip Sousa as much as the next guy, but tuba and sousaphone melodies are not conducive to a successful ghost hunt; we would have to delay until the concert was finished.

With time on my hands, I was able to walk around the front yard, admiring the Prussian blue columns of the front porch and the trim of the six-over-six windows set neatly in the brick walls. Inside the house, Melinda and some of her team members were setting up their gear. After a few minutes I went inside to join them and was pleasantly surprised to see Cheryl Crowell, an old friend with whom I had lost touch and had not seen for nearly ten years, who was now affiliated with the nonprofit that owned the house and would be on the investigation with us.

Also inside the house was Greg Roberts, a local historian who knew everything there was to know about the house and the city of New Richmond. Greg gave me a chronology of all the past owners of the house—always good to have when trying to uncover the identity of the resident ghosts—but there didn't seem to be any murders, suicides, or other acts of violence and mayhem that often result in hauntings. With the exception of the periodic floods, life at Ross Gowdy House appeared to be peaceful and serene. But peaceful and serene could be good hunting grounds for ghosts, too: there is a theory that ghosts haunt the places where they were happiest in life. The Ross Gowdy House could be such a place for those ghosts. I wondered if the house, so close to the river, could have been a stop on the Underground Railroad, but Greg didn't think there was any evidence to support that.

"So, what exactly goes on here?" I asked. We were standing in the front parlor off the entrance hall. Melinda was adjusting a monitor she was setting up on a table in the corner. Behind the table stood a beautiful, ornately carved organ.

Melinda turned to me. "For one thing, there was a sighting of a woman dressed in white in the upstairs bedroom window," she said.

"In a 1937 flood, there was a trapped woman who was rescued from that window," Greg said. "She was old, though, and died from a heart attack."

"And that's the ghost?" I asked.

"It could be," said Melinda. "We don't know for sure."

Cheryl said that she felt shivers and had the strange sense of another presence in the house when she was working there alone. She said that the alarms in the house go off without anyone being there and that lights blink on and off.

Other people have experienced cold spots in the house and have heard disembodied footsteps and loud knocking on the walls. A former occupant renting the upstairs rooms felt someone in a dress brush by her and saw the curtain at the windows moving. Someone saw an apparition of a woman in a white dress standing in the doorway of an upstairs bedroom whispering, *I promise.*

When the band's last "oompah" finally sounded and the crowd dispersed, we set about getting the investigation under way—it was almost 10:30. Melinda's team had placed some cameras in different parts of the house, both upstairs and down, so the monitor on the table now showed four areas inside the house simultaneously. While those cameras filmed throughout the night the rest of us would work in small groups in the various rooms with handheld equipment.

The house was not very large; a small parlor off the hall on the ground floor and a larger dining room with an elegant fireplace mantel at the end of the hall. A tiny kitchen was to one side of the dining room, and a little bedroom with a four-poster bed occupying most of the space was located at the rear of the house. The curved staircase led to two empty rooms on the second floor, one of them taking up the entire front of the house.

Because a ghost had been seen by the window in the front room upstairs, a S.O.A.R. team member spread a plastic garbage bag on the floor beneath the window and sprinkled it with white powder in hopes of recording spectral footprints if a ghost decided to climb out—or in, I suppose—through the window.

Several of us gathered in the upstairs front room. Melinda placed a tray on the floor and upon that placed an antique musical shaker, an old baby shoe, a compass, an antique desk-bell, and a lighted candle. She also sat an EMF meter and a K2 meter on the tray. Throughout the night Melinda, or any of us, would ask the ghosts to make use of the various objects on the tray; ring the bell, blow out the candle, rattle the shaker. The EMF and K2 meters would hopefully capture their responses. I liked the idea of giving the ghosts something to play with, something to do; the afterlife appears to be a boring place.

Ross Gowdy House organ

We had all the windows in the house open since the temperature inside was in the high 80s but, unfortunately, there were still late-night revelers in the park and street outside and the noise they were making was interfering with our recordings. After about an hour of that, we shut the windows. Even so, when we reviewed the data later on, we found that the first hour's worth of recordings were useless because there was so much outside interference. Such are the pitfalls of ghosthunting.

In the upstairs room we sat on the floor, placing the tray with the various objects in the center of the room. We began to ask the typical questions of the spirits:

Is there anyone here that would like to speak to us?
Can you tell us your name?
Do you know what year it is?
Can you tell us how old you are?

We did not expect to get an audible answer to any of these questions but we did hope that our recorders would pick up a ghostly reply that we would hear on playback. We continued to ask questions, trying to focus on questions that required more than a simple "yes-no" reply.

There is a theory that says ghosts drain whatever energy they can get from the environment in order to "live." This explains why ghosthunters so often complain about brand-new batteries in cameras, flashlights, recorders, etc., going dead right away; the ghosts have drained that energy. I believe that theory also explains "cold spots" in haunted locations. If ghosts drain energy from the environment, wouldn't they also drain thermal (heat) energy? If they did draw that energy—literally sucking the heat out of a room—you would experience a cold spot or a drop in room temperature.

Perhaps with that theory in mind, Melinda asked the ghost if it could drop the temperature in the room. Using a remote digital thermometer, we recorded the room temperature at 85 degrees.

"Can you lower the temperature?" Melinda asked the dark.

We sat there quietly, waiting.

"Make it colder if you can," Melinda said.

We waited.

After a few minutes someone said that they felt a breeze.

"My arms are getting cold," Melinda said.

That's when I felt a stream of cool air against my arm. I was wearing a short-sleeved shirt and could clearly feel the draft. "I'm getting a draft blowing against my arm," I said.

"Does anyone else feel anything?" Melinda asked.

One of the other team members, Tanya, said she felt a draft as well.

The breeze on my arm was stronger now, actually cold. I was sitting near the doorway to the room, so I leaned over to that area and reached out into the darkness to see if I felt a breeze there. Maybe it was a natural breeze from outside, coming up the stairwell, I thought. Nothing. The air was still and hot. Moving back into my original position, I once again felt the draft, colder than ever.

"It's still here," I said. "Colder now."

"OK" said Melinda. "My arms are freezing."

I scooted back a few inches to see if I could discover the source of the draft, even though I knew the windows behind me were closed and, without air-conditioning in the house, there was no way to explain that frosty draft.

"My arms are so cold!" Melinda said. "Someone get a temperature reading."

In the darkness I couldn't tell who was using the thermometer, but I saw the red laser eye flash on in my direction and then heard someone say, "Seventy-eight degrees."

Seventy-eight! Great Caesar's ghost! The room temperature had dropped seven degrees for no apparent reason. The only explanation we had was that Melinda has asked the ghost to lower the temperature, and I guess it did.

It took a few minutes for the temperature to drop and while it was dropping, we also heard strange sounds coming from the room adjacent to the bedroom in which we were gathered. There were shuffling sounds, as though someone were moving around in the dark; popping sounds one might hear on old wooden floorboards; and knocking on walls. Sometimes these sounds would occur immediately after a question was asked, as if in reply.

After several minutes the temperature rose once more and

we were not able to get the ghost to lower it again. We concluded our investigation upstairs and moved down to the bedroom at the rear of the house. During a previous S.O.A.R. investigation, a guest investigator asked, *Is this the bedroom you stay in?* The recording captured a female voice responding, *But, I don't.* It seemed that the bedroom would be a good place to conduct another EVP session.

Melinda placed the same objects she had used upstairs on the bed and once again invited the ghost to use any of them. The rest of us gathered around the bed, asking questions, waiting for answers. At one point, it seemed that the compass needle moved a few degrees, but we thought that someone had bumped up against the bed, jiggling the compass.

We continued asking questions for quite some time but did not hear audible responses of any kind. Early in the morning, we concluded the investigation.

Later, upon review of the data we found that we had recorded several EVPs. In the upstairs bedroom, a female voice said, *Help me*, followed by a childlike, whispered *Help.* Also upstairs, Melinda asks, "Maybe they will ring the bell?" followed by a man saying, *Can't.* At one point, while we were all downstairs, we had left a recorder switched on upstairs. That recorder picked up breathing sounds and *Yes.*

There is no question that the historic Ross Gowdy House has a ghost or two still living in it. Who the ghosts are remains a mystery, one you might be lucky enough to unravel.

Legendary Ghosts: Enos Kay

Back in the nineteenth century a young man named Enos Kay lived along Egypt Pike in Ross County. Enos was an honest, hard-working young man who had become the envy of the county since he won the affections of Alvira the local beauty.

It took several years of scrimping and saving for Enos to get together enough money for a wedding worthy of his beloved Alvira. But at last he had the money, and soon wedding arrangements were under way. The wedding clothes were being fashioned, and everything was going well for the young couple until the fateful day in 1869 when they decided to attend a church picnic.

A mysterious stranger, a man none of the churchgoers had ever seen, showed up at the church picnic that day. It was even unclear what the man called himself; some of the picnickers thought his name was Smith, while others thought it was Johnston, or maybe Brown. One thing they all agreed upon was that the man clearly had eyes for the beautiful Alvira. Throughout the day, the stranger did his best to woo the girl while meek and hapless Enos simply stood by and watched.

It wasn't long before rumors began to circulate that Alvira had been seen walking hand in hand with the handsome stranger, rumors that Enos simply dismissed as idle chatter. How could the love of his life, the woman who had promised her love to him, be with another man? Impossible. But when Enos heard a few days later that the man had climbed through Alvira's bedroom window at night and proposed to her, and that she had accepted and run off with the man, he was stunned.

Enos immediately ran to his fiancée's house, where he discovered, much to his grief, that Alvira had, indeed, jilted him and was gone forever. Enos let out a heart-breaking cry and swore that he would forever haunt happy lovers until Judgment Day. Then, he

Legendary Ghosts: Enos Kay
(continued)

walked out to Timmons Bridge, the local lovers' lane, and hanged himself from the rafters.

Not long after Enos's body was committed to the ground came the frightening stories of lovers being terrorized at the bridge by some unseen force. Couples reported an invisible force attacking their buggies, shaking them violently, and spooking the horses. Some couples said that the malevolent force ripped open the tops of the buggies, revealing the demonic face of Enos Kay peering down at them.

Encounters with the ghost of Enos Kay are reported to this day. Apparently, he will not bother lone motorists passing over the bridge, or a parked couple who are arguing instead of kissing. True to his oath, the ghost claws and scratches at the parked cars of those couples who are expressing their ardor. Some of these "couples interruptus" recall seeing the ghost's devilish grin through the steamed car windows. The moral here might be, *Get a room!*

Spotlight On: The Ghost of Englewood Dam

While I was doing some research at the Dayton Metro Library, I met Nancy Horlacher, the Local History Specialist. She was interested in my project and e-mailed me a story titled "The Phantom Driver on Englewood Dam," from the manuscript entitled *Tales and Sketches of the Great Miami Valley*, by Earl Leon Heck, written in 1962.

Mr. Heck reports on a strange and disturbing vision that terrorized truckers in the winter of 1952 as they drove their rigs on the road that crosses the Englewood Dam. The road was narrow, flanked by wooden guardrails on either side, with a precipitous 125-foot drop-off should a driver become careless or sleepy.

Heck writes that on a stormy, icy night that winter a seasoned trucker named Roy Fitzwater stopped at a small inn located near the dam, a favorite stop for drivers. He was shaken and visibly distraught but refused to answer any of his fellow truckers' questions, stating only that he had witnessed something "quite horrible." Ohio Highway Patrol Officer Harrell was also eating at the inn and knew Fitzwater. He asked the trucker what was wrong but Fitzwater simply shook his head and declined to say anything more, eventually leaving the inn without revealing anything.

Over the next few weeks, three more truck drivers stopped at the inn as frightened as Fitzwater, but none of them would talk about what they had experienced. Officer Harrell happened to be at the inn each time and saw these seasoned, professional masters of the road reduced to nervous, scared children. About a month later, Roy Fitzwater stopped at the inn and Officer Harrell was once again present—you have to believe that Harrell needed a lot of coffee to keep himself going since he was so often at the inn. This time the patrolman convinced Fitzwater to tell his story.

Spotlight On: The Ghost of Englewood Dam
(continued)

Fitzwater said that while he was crossing the dam on a dark, stormy night, car headlights suddenly appeared in the opposite direction heading toward his truck." It comes straight toward me, with blinding lights," the trucker said, "just as if he intended to plunge right into me."

Fitzwater told Harrell that he slammed on the brakes and tried to swerve out of the way, knowing that if he was not careful, he could drive his rig over the side of the dam. When the car was only about 200 feet away it turned across the truck's path.

"The lights go out," Fitzwater continued, "but inside the car appears a dull blue-green light of the most unearthly kind, revealing a skull and skeleton at the wheel. You can see the bones all lighted up with this peculiar, uncanny light. It is just too horrible to describe. It just about takes the life out of you."

Harrell and other patrolmen staked out the dam and the road, but the phantom driver was never seen again after that horrific winter in 1952. Perhaps he's driving other highways of America's Haunted Road Trip.

CHAPTER 4

Snow Hill Country Club
NEW VIENNA

WHEN I FIRST HEARD THAT Snow Hill Country Club in New Vienna was haunted, I had visions of ghosts madly driving golf carts over the fairways and spectral golfers breaking spectral clubs over spectral knees after shanking spectral Titleists into the very real woods. As it turned out, I wasn't that far off.

Originally built as an inn in 1820 by Charles and Catherine Harris, who had moved to Clinton County from Snow Hill, Maryland, Snow Hill quickly gained an excellent reputation and was frequented by many a weary traveler. In 1840, the inn hosted the famous Philadelphia Circus; it also served as a polling place for forty years. But, as so often happened with many of America's old inns, modern forms of transportation, especially railroads, meant fewer and fewer customers at Snow Hill. In 1898, the inn was sold at auction and became a storage place for grain. The elegant old structure began to fall into disrepair until the early 1900s when Norma Harris, the granddaughter of Charles and Catherine, bought the inn, renovated and expanded it, and opened it in 1924 as Snow Hill Country Club.

At the invitation of Steven Powell of the Ohio Organization for Paranormal Studies (O.O.P.S.) I found myself driving through a torrential downpour one July night to join the O.O.P.S. team for an investigation at Snow Hill. The rain sluiced over my car and the country roads were narrow and hilly, all of which made driving a nightmare. At one point, I drove through the sprawling and abandoned DHL airport facility, where the ghosts of 10,000 lost jobs still lingered. At another point, I missed a turn in the deluge, ended up at a dead end, and had to reroute myself. Even my GPS was confused. Finally, I pulled into the parking lot beside the white-columned clubhouse, thinking to myself, if the trip out here was any indication of what was to come, it was going to be a wild night.

Steven gave me a quick tour of the premises, which included the original 1820 building—now completely restored with a bar, dining room, and guest rooms—and the 1920s addition of locker rooms, card rooms, and meeting rooms.

Steven told me that O.O.P.S. (I love that name!) was formed three years ago and that they conducted paranormal investigations primarily in the Wilmington area. Over the years the group had become Snow Hill's "house band," and they routinely conducted investigations there and also sponsored a "Dinner and a Ghost" event each October.

"So, tell me what you've experienced," I said to Steven, as we stood in an empty dining area.

He pointed to the old doors of the room and said that the door latches sometimes move on their own, as if some invisible being was seeking admittance. In that same room, an antique candle maker fastened to the wall came off all by itself.

"We've also recorded a lot of EVPs in the building," Steven said, referring to mysterious voices and sounds picked up on recorders but inaudible to investigators at the time they were recorded. The voices are believed to be those of spirits.

We walked into the lounge, where Steven pointed out rows of glassware on shelves behind the bar. There wasn't anything out of the ordinary about them that I could see, but Steven said that one night the glasses in a back row lifted up and over the glasses in the front row. I went behind the bar to take a closer look at the shelves and I could see no way that such a thing could happen without human intervention.

As we were talking, more O.O.P.S. members drifted in and began setting up the investigation, running cables throughout the building and positioning cameras and recorders in various rooms. Steven had previous obligations and would not be staying for the investigation, but I would be working with the rest of the team: Tom, Scott, Steven's daughter Jennifer, Chanda, and Andrea.

The O.O.P.S. team was well organized and seemed to have everything under control. Steven had already prepared a map of the building on which the team could mark the placement of the equipment . . . and they had a *ton* of electronic gear. For the most part, I just tried to stay out of their way as they set up.

I took a walk up the steep staircase to the second floor where the guest rooms were located. Although the rooms had recently been remodeled, everything was made to look much as it would have looked during the inn's nineteenth-century heyday. High ceilings with ornate molding, colorful wallpapers, beautiful stone and wood hearths, paintings in elaborate gilt frames, and

Snow Hill Country Club and O.O.P.S. founder Steven Powell

period-style furniture all helped to turn back the clock in these beautiful rooms.

I stepped into Room Three, a smaller room with a bed angled in a corner near the door. This room was said to be the most paranormally active of the guest rooms. A guest who was sleeping in the room suddenly awoke because he was getting wet from what he called a "leaking ceiling." When the staff checked out the room, however, they found no leaks, no water. Also in that room, the team had previously recorded an EVP saying *Don't tell nothing.*

Returning back downstairs after a few minutes I found that the team was ready to go. The dining room was the "command center," with a monitor set up on which we could view four different areas of the clubhouse simultaneously. We would switch off and on during the night, but at all times there would be at least one person watching the monitor. The rest of us would work in small teams, investigating the various rooms of the clubhouse.

Before we started, Scott and ponytailed Tom went into the lounge and turned on some music. Rap music. It sounded something like *Yo bee-otch, I'm a bad @!#* and I'm gonna *!^#@ you like you ain't never been *!^#@ cuz I be *&%@# with my #@*%$ and @#@!%$ with your #!*&#*. It seemed funny to me to see these two big, burly, Midwestern white guys hip-hopping to mo-fo music, but they explained it to me by saying that such "energetic" music helped to stir up the environment, to create some energy for the ghosts to make their presence known; the science of ghosthunting is unorthodox, to say the least.

But the commonly held theory about ghosts is that they need to draw energy to "live," and they will take it from wherever they can get it. This theory helps to explain why rainy and stormy nights, like the night of our investigation, often result in more paranormal activity than other nights, as all the energy generated by such weather is conducive to ghostly manifestations.

I spent most of the evening working with Tom and Scott. We would go into various rooms with cameras and recorders and spend some time there trying to make contact with the spirits. Since O.O.P.S. had recorded EVPs at Snow Hill in the past, we were hopeful we would get some that night but, of course, we wouldn't know if we were successful until after we reviewed all the data later.

On one of their previous investigations, the O.O.P.S. team video recorded a door swinging open on its own accord in the men's locker room. That video is on the O.O.P.S. website; it's pretty impressive. Hoping to recapture such a moment or maybe to experience something even better, we spent a good part of the night in the locker room. The three of us sat scattered in the dark locker room, visible to each other only by the little lights on our cameras and recorders. One of us would speak into the darkness, asking questions of the unseen spirits and then quietly wait for a response we hoped could be picked up on our recorders. Every now and then we would hear a faint sound, perhaps a tap, or maybe a footstep, and our senses would come to full alert, but we could not conclusively say that those sounds were of a paranormal nature.

A card room adjoined the men's locker room, and after try-ing our luck in the locker room for awhile we moved to the card room. We sat around the card table and, once again, asked our questions. For the sake of accurate documentation of the data, we would always speak into the recorder the names of the investiga-tors in the room and our location. Tom spoke into his recorder, "This is John, Tom, and Scott in the men's card room."

It was about 4 a.m., and it was difficult not to nod off as we sat at the table, asking questions now and then but mostly sitting quietly in the dark, allowing the ghosts their chance to speak. This passive—and to be frank, boring—part of ghost-hunting is rarely shown on television, where ghosts seem to pop up at every turn. They don't.

I'm not sure how long we remained there—I don't think that I fell asleep—but after some time we decided to end our session in the card room and headed back to the command center. We compared notes with the women, and it seemed that none of us had experienced any tangible evidence of ghosts that night. I stayed there for a little bit, taking a turn at the monitor while some of the others went back out. Keeping in mind my arduous trek out to Snow Hill and the late hour, I decided to leave about half an hour later.

I was not part of the group that reviewed all the video and audio data that we had collected, but about two weeks after my visit to Snow Hill, Steven Powell contacted me to tell me what they had discovered. Maybe it was the weather or the nasty rap music that gave the ghosts what they needed to communicate with us that night, but it seems that they were quite talkative.

Chanda, Andrea, and Jennifer were upstairs in Room 2 off the main hallway when they recorded a male voice saying *I'm sorry.* This voice was recorded both on a recorder that was placed in the hall and on Andrea's handheld recorder.

Two other EVPs recorded in that area are again male voices saying *work* and what sounds like *the song of Satan,* which may have been a response to a question asked about the rap music. (I know that's what I would say about it if I were a ghost.)

But the EVP that impressed me the most was the one that Tom picked up on his handheld recorder while we sat at the table in the men's card room. Just as Tom, Scott, and I were leaving the basement, and barely a minute before Tom switched off his recorder, a male voice said, *This is John (pause), Ike (pause), Edward.* What is startling about this EVP is that it is almost an exact repetition of what Tom had said when we first settled ourselves in the card room, although, with the exception of *John,* the names were different. Was the ghost mimicking us, only with a faulty memory? Were there three ghosts in that room named John, Ike, and Edward? Was I the *John* the ghost was talking about? I heard that EVP and my name is whispered in a ghostly male voice clear as a bell.

Less than twenty seconds after that EVP, Tom's recorder picked up a male voice saying, *Look at me.* Of course, all that night we *were* looking into the darkness, hoping to see beyond the veil that separates our world from the spirit world. It seems as though the ghost wanted to be seen as badly as we wanted to see him. It didn't work that time, but the ghosts of Snow Hill seem to want to cooperate, so maybe some other day?

Spotlight On: D.O.G.S.

Brothers Rob and Ed Fremder founded the Dayton Ohio Ghosthunters Society (D.O.G.S.) in late 2007. By 2011, in its fourth year of investigating the paranormal in the Dayton area, D.O.G.S. had expanded its membership from eight to more than a dozen active members. D.O.G.S. is by no means a group of "ghost busters" and they make no claims about being able to remove spirits from a haunted location. The group makes a concerted effort toward figuring out what is haunting the location, what the entity wants, advising on how to deal with spirits, and discovering alternate explanations that may explain the observed phenomena. D.O.G.S. also does property research, including deed transfers resulting from a death.

The group's favorite haunted location is the Poasttown Elementary School just north of Middletown. They have investigated there more than a half dozen times and have gotten great evidence each time.

The group's website is **daytonghs.org**, and they also have social networking pages on Facebook at **facebook.com/dayton ghs** and on MySpace at **myspace.com/daytonohioghs**.

CHAPTER 5

Promont House Museum
MILFORD

BUILT BETWEEN 1865 AND 1867, this beautiful Italianate-style mansion was nicknamed "McGrue's Folly" because the owner, William G. McGrue, spent a mind-boggling $48,000 for its construction and located it in the middle of nowhere, also known as Milford, Ohio. Originally situated on fifty acres, the house—now a historical museum and the home of the Greater

Milford Area Historical Society—sits on five acres of beautiful mature trees and gardens. The house is distinguished by its imposing five-story tower that leads from the basement up to an observation room at the summit.

When John M. Pattison bought the house in 1879, his wife, Aletheia, named it Promont. She and Pattison had four children, but Aletheia died in the house only a few years after moving into it. In 1893, Pattison married Anna Williams, his first wife's sister. Pattison led a distinguished career in Ohio business and politics and in 1906 was elected as Ohio's forty-third governor. Unfortunately, the trials of the campaign had weakened his constitution, and after giving his inaugural speech in January 1906 during a snowstorm, he fell ill with pneumonia. Unable to attend legislative sessions in the state house, he conducted the affairs of state from his home. But his health continued to decline; on June 18 of that year, Governor Pattison died at Promont.

The mansion eventually passed into the hands of millionaire tobacco farmer Henry Hodges. The Hodges occupied the home for forty years, and both Henry and his wife died at Promont.

When Promont was built, it was a technological marvel. The mansion featured gas lighting, central heat from a coal-fired furnace, call bells, and a gravity flow running water system. Today, the elegant home has been restored to how it looked during Governor Pattison's residency, and it is filled with Victorian furniture and artifacts.

I visited Promont in October. It was a beautiful, warm Indian summer day, and the trees on the grounds blazed in autumn colors of scarlet and gold. Parking my car in the visitors' lot I stood there for a moment, admiring the house and its magnificent tower shining in the sunlight. It was obvious why the locals called it a "folly"—it would have been much more at home on a hillside overlooking vineyards in Tuscany than it was in Milford, a mere stone's throw from the semis roaring down I-275.

I went around to the entrance, walked up the stone steps of the porch, and pushed open one of the massive but elegant wooden doors, each set with a large window. When I entered the center hall foyer, a docent named Bill (real name withheld by request) invited me to join him and another visitor on a guided tour of the house, which I did.

It is always difficult to describe the grand old homes I visit, so full are they of intricate architectural details, fine furnishings, and artwork. Promont was no exception. High-ceilinged rooms ornamented with plaster crown molding and lamp medallions in the form of garlands, wreaths, and fruit, all of them hand-crafted and painted; stately pocket doors at least eight feet tall, maybe taller; ornate crystal chandeliers; a glowing "Tree of Life" stained glass window at the top of the first floor landing; and, of course, the architectural centerpiece of the house, the gracefully winding staircase that led from the basement up to the small glass-enclosed observation room five stories above the ground. What always amazes me in houses like Promont is the artistic craftsmanship that went into creating all these wonderful details. They seem to be lost arts today or, if available at all, tagged with an excrbitant cost affordable only be sheikhs from Dubai.

In addition to the period furniture that graced the rooms of Promont there were historical exhibits on display. Photos, letters, and other memorabilia displayed in the center hall related the history of local residents who fought in the Civil War. Upstairs, just a few steps below the observation room, was a large room filled with antique clothing, tools, and appliances, a smorgasbord of historical artifacts. The stairwell was also lined with photos and maps of historical interest.

Viewing all those photos and artifacts, walking through the heart of a house that was almost 150 years old, it was easy to step back in time, to feel what it would have been like to have been

**Promont House Tree of Life
stained glass window**

a Pattison family member living there in that beautiful and serene home. Since ghosts often remain at the places at which they were the happiest, it would seem to me that Promont would be a perfect candidate for such a spiritual haven.

So, it should come as no surprise to find out that, according to a number of people, Promont is haunted.

The tower staircase seems to be one area in which paranormal activity occurs. People who work at Promont have reported hearing footsteps walking up the stairs from the bottom all the way to the top, or in the opposite direction, with each deliberate step resounding loudly.

One story says that a librarian working in the historical society's library upstairs heard someone coming up the steps from the ground floor. The librarian called down to tell the person that the house was closed, but the footsteps continued coming up the stairs. She ran out to the top of the stairs, but there was no one to be seen and the footsteps stopped when she arrived. The frightened librarian then made a hasty exit out the back door.

Another woman working at the house once felt someone or something grab her ankle. She asked her coworker why she had done that, but the other woman denied having touched her.

Other people have reported cabinets, shutters, and doors at the house opening and closing on their own.

Richard Crawford is a Clermont County historian who has studied many local strange and haunted locations. One of the places he talks about on his DVD, *True Ghost Stories from Ohio*, is Promont. Crawford says that a nurse who worked for the man who last owned the house would not go down to the basement because of strange sounds coming from there, the sounds of something moving around. He also says that other visitors to Promont, such as plumbers, electricians, etc., refuse to go down to the basement or will not go there alone because of the unsettling sounds. These tradesmen, no doubt, often work in old houses and must be accustomed to the sounds that naturally occur in such homes—creaking floors, popping sounds from expanding and contracting wood, radiator noises, hissing steam pipes, knocking sounds in heating and cooling ductwork, wind moaning through drafty walls and windows among them—but they don't refuse to work in those houses, so what is it about the sounds in the basement at Promont that has them so spooked? Could it be that on some visceral level they recognize those sounds as paranormal, or out of the ordinary? Ghostly?

Who is the ghost that is haunting Promont? Many people think it is Gov. John Pattison who still roams the halls of his beloved Promont, checking things out, making sure everything is running smoothly at his former home. In addition to the grand staircase, much of the paranormal activity in the house seems to center on the master bedroom on the second floor. It is believed that Pattison drew his last breath in this room, so such activity might be expected there.

Whether the ghost is that of Governor Pattison or someone else remains a mystery. The evidence suggests that *someone* is haunting the beautiful Promont house. Perhaps you might be the first to uncover the true identity of the ghost.

Spotlight On: The Ghosts of Utopia

In 1844 a man named Charles Fourier bought property in Clermont County along the Ohio River. Fourier was a member of a religious sect that believed the world was entering a 35,000-year period of peace. In his futuristic vision all of the world's peoples would be collected into "phalanxes," communes of a sort. Fourier also believed the oceans would turn into lemonade—no joke. Even with his lemonade theory, Fourier was able to attract more than a dozen families to his own phalanx, which he named Utopia.

For a rent of $25 a year, each family received a wooden house. Fourier's plans called for the community to eventually have its own farmland, stables, schools, and libraries. Fourier built a community dining hall on the river and a thirty-room brick house on higher ground.

Fourier's followers were patient but when the oceans did not turn into lemonade as he had predicted, many became disillusioned and left the community. In 1847, Fourier sold the property and buildings to John O. Wattles, a Spiritualist leader. The first thing Wattles did was to move the brick building down to the riverbank, brick by brick. It was rebuilt by December of that year, just in time for the record floods that washed through the Ohio River valley, bringing with them record-breaking high water.

Despite all warnings, many of the Spiritualists gathered in the brick house for a dance on the night of December 12. The party came to a gruesome end, though, when the bricks gave way in the rushing flood waters and many of the people inside were swept away into the dark and freezing waters.

Today, Utopia is little more than two roads that dead-end at the river, a gas station, and a couple houses. But some say the Spiritualists are still there. There are reports of soggy apparitions coming up out of the river or walking along the riverbank.

Spotlight On: The Ghosts of Utopia
(continued)

Also, an underground stone chamber still remains on the banks of the river. It opens to the surface in two places that are fenced in, but that has not stopped people from climbing over and then descending into the chamber. About twenty feet deep, the dirt-floored chamber has a vaulted roof and two fireplaces. No one knows for certain who built the chamber or how it was used. Was it Wattle's Spiritualist church? A stop on the Underground Railroad? An old storage facility? Whatever it may have been, it makes an excellent hiding place for ghosts.

Two young men were driving along the river one night when they spotted the *Utopia* sign. Curious about the place, they stopped to investigate. There wasn't much to see, but as they picked their way along the riverbank in the dark the men saw a white shape in the distance, coming toward them. As it drew closer they saw that it was taking on a more recognizable form, that of an old woman dressed in tattered clothes. One of the men ran back to the car to get his camera, but by the time he got back, the old woman had disappeared. Was she one of Wattle's drowned followers?

Maybe you can find out for yourself. The next time you're driving on SR 52 in Clermont County, make sure you stop at Utopia and spend some time with its ghosts.

Northwest

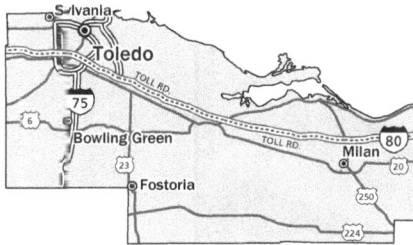

Bowling Green
Wood County Historical Center & Museum

Milan
Thomas Edison Birthplace

Sylvania
Jenna's Mediterranean Restaurant

Toledo
Oliver House

CHAPTER 6

Jenna's Mediterranean Restaurant

SYLVANIA

MY WIFE, MARY, AND I WERE IN SYLVANIA because I was giving a talk about ghosts and ghosthunting at Our Lady of Lourdes College. I'm always amazed at the variety of places that invite me to speak about ghosts, but that's proof of just how popular ghosts and ghost stories are these days.

Before my talk we were taking in the sights of downtown Sylvania when we happened upon Jenna's Mediterranean Restaurant on Main Street. We stepped inside for a late lunch. When we read *Your taste is my command* on the menus, we knew we were in the right place. I had hummus with beef tips and Mary had the chicken *shawarma,* both of which were excellent, but the baklava we had for dessert was the best baklava I've had anywhere and, believe me, over the years I've eaten my fair share of baklava! We complimented our waitress, Angie, on the good food. One thing led to another, and I told her about my book and why I was in town. To my surprise—although it happens so often that I really shouldn't be surprised anymore—Angie told me that the restaurant was haunted. She suggested I talk to the owner, who was not in but would be in the morning.

That evening I gave my talk at the college, and in the morning I went over to Jenna's. The restaurant wasn't open for business yet, but the owner, Jerry Assad, was already getting things ready for the lunch crowd. Jerry was a young, energetic guy, trying to make it big in the competitive restaurant business with a restaurant named for his beloved, deceased daughter—I have no doubts that he will be successful.

While he was busily working in the kitchen he told me that, yes, the place was haunted. He wiped his hands on a towel and steered me over to a small table where a framed newspaper article was prominently displayed. He picked it up and handed it to me.

"This article will tell you all about the haunting," Jerry said.

I began to read the article, and it did start off with the haunting at Jenna's, including a few quotes from Jerry. But as I continued to read I found that the reporter expanded the article to include other Ohio ghosts and was now talking about me and my work, including some quotes from my books! Jerry was as surprised as I was to find my name mentioned in the article.

"So, this restaurant was the scene of a murder?" I asked Jerry.

"Yes, it seems that it took place in this building," he said. He handed me a book titled *Murder in Sylvania, Ohio: As Told in 1857* by Gage E. Gindy, who had collected and compiled all the newspaper accounts of one of Ohio's most gruesome crimes. "This book really tells the story," Jerry said.

I sat down at one of the tables and perused the book. According to the newspaper accounts, on February 3, 1857, Olive Ward told her husband, Return Jonathan Meigs Ward, that she was leaving him for good (they had already been separated). That day was the last time anyone ever saw Olive alive. As people searched for her and rumors began to fly about her disappearance, suspicions fell on Return Ward. Could he have done away with poor Olive? A policeman came to the house to interrogate Ward but found no evidence of any crime committed (later testimony from Ward revealed that, while the policeman was in the house, parts of Olive's body were in a box under the couch).

Despite that initial lack of evidence, the police remained suspicious of Ward, and on a subsequent search of the house discovered bits of human bone in the ashes Ward had thrown out from the fireplace. There were also bones found in the stove. It appeared that Ward had murdered his wife, cut her body up into pieces, and then burned them.

Ward was arrested and tried. He was found guilty and admitted his guilt. Moreover, he confessed to two other murders in Richland County. On June 12, 1857, Ward, Ohio's first serial killer, was hanged at the Lucas County Courthouse in Toledo. His last words were, "Oh, my God, I am thine. Thou art mine."

I put the book down and looked around the dining room. Early in the day yet, there were no patrons. It was a pleasant place and it was difficult for me to visualize such a heinous crime taking place there. It was difficult to imagine the screams of poor Olive as her husband hacked her to death. But Jerry is certain that the strange events taking place at Jenna's are caused by the restless spirits caught up in that crime so long ago. And Jerry is not alone in that belief.

He told me that he once had a waitress who had gone into the ladies' room. It was 3:30 in the afternoon. Suddenly, he heard what sounded like three loud gunshots. At the same time, the waitress in the ladies' room saw the lock on the door turn, the door opened by itself, and then slammed shut; two other doors in the hallway where the ladies' room is located also slammed shut. Jerry said that the terrified waitress came running out to the kitchen "with her pants around her knees." She quit and has never been back to Jenna's since that day.

Jerry said that people often feel breezes blowing through the hallway by the ladies' room, even when all the doors are closed. I examined the hallway and went inside the bathroom to check the lock and the door. They both worked fine. I could see no way that the lock would turn by itself or that the door would open or close without human intervention. The hallway exits at the rear of the restaurant where there is another door to the outside, and I thought the slamming doors might have been caused by air pressure from the outside door but again, examining that door, I could not see how that would be possible.

There are other paranormal occurrences at Jenna's. Jerry said that when he was first renovating the restaurant, he heard music coming out of the walls. "It was old saloon kind of music," he said. "That's exactly what it sounded like."

Jerry once felt a presence standing near him and heard someone clearing his throat; he was alone at the time. He has also heard footsteps running up and down the hallway and the sound of giggling children. He has heard those same sounds in the basement as well.

As we were talking, two of the waitstaff, Angie and Joe,

came into the restaurant and set about their tasks. Angie was working at the bar, and I went over to talk with her. The day before, she hadn't said anything about her ghostly experiences at Jenna's—perhaps waiting to get the go-ahead from Jerry— but after seeing me talking with her boss she felt more comfortable in relating her story.

I asked what she had witnessed at the restaurant. She set down some glasses on the bar and looked around the room for a moment, almost as though she expected to see a ghost. "I've seen things here," she said, looking at me. "I've seen black figures walking through the dining room."

I got the impression from Angie that she thought at least some of them were female; Olive Ward?

"Not just me," Angie continued. "Other waitresses have seen the same black figures here in the dining room and in the kitchen as well."

Just behind me, the young waiter Joe was setting a table. I turned to him. "What about you, Joe? Have you ever seen anything unusual here?"

He stopped, knives and forks clutched in his hands. "I haven't seen those figures," he said, "but I did have a very strange thing happen to me. I had just set up some tables, and I had pushed all the chairs in close to the table. I turned away for a moment, and I felt this cold breeze suddenly go by. When I turned back to the table all the chairs were pulled away from it."

"That's weird," I said.

Joe nodded. "But that's not all. There were now wine glasses set at each of the places."

"And you didn't put them there," I said.

"No, I didn't."

Such an experience would be enough to unnerve me, but I guess Joe felt the ghosts were helping him with his work—and he wouldn't even have to tip them.

Jerry was chopping and dicing in the kitchen, and I went back to talk with him. I asked him about the figures in the kitchen and he said that yes, several people had seen them. Did they interact with any of the staff, I asked him, and he replied that they did not.

"Not like the health inspector," he said, barely concealing a smile.

"The health inspector?" I asked.

"Come with me," he said, putting down the knife and wiping his hands. "I want to show you something."

I followed Jerry through the hall to the basement door. We went downstairs, switching on the lights as we went. The basement was what you would imagine any restaurant basement to look like; a tiny, messy "office," supplies stacked up wherever there was free space, a washing machine for table linens, and a large freezer. Jerry stopped in front of the freezer. It was tall and large enough for a person to walk inside.

"This was where the health inspector met the ghost," he said.

"Really? What happened?"

"He came down here on a routine inspection," Jerry said, "and went into the freezer. He was down there for a few minutes, too long I thought, so I went down to check on him and heard him banging from inside the freezer and calling to be let out. I opened the door and let him out."

The inspector said that after he had gone inside the freezer the door slammed shut behind him and the light inside the freezer went out. He tried the handle but it was locked and he found himself trapped in the freezer.

"How did it get locked from the inside?" I asked.

Jerry smiled. "That's a good question," he said, "especially when there is no lock. I couldn't lock the freezer if I tried."

"What do you mean?"

"There's no lock," Jerry repeated. "Check for yourself."

I went to the freezer and tried the handle. Sure enough, there was no lock on it. No one could possibly get locked inside the freezer.

But tell that to the health inspector.

No one knows for sure if the mysterious figures and the inexplicable events at Jenna's have anything to do with the murder of Olive Ward, but I'm betting that they do, at least some of them. Other people agree with me. Jerry told me about the mysterious old man who came to the restaurant shortly after it opened. He cryptically told Jerry about strange happenings in the basement and then said, *Mrs. Ward has won out.*

Maybe she has. Make a visit to Jenna's restaurant and find out for yourself; and do yourself a favor—have a piece of Jerry's baklava.

What's in a Name?
Crybaby Bridge

It seems that almost every state has a haunted bridge nicknamed Crybaby Bridge, and the hauntings are all similar to each other. All of them have to do with the death of a child, or the mother and child. There are several Crybaby Bridges in Ohio:

ABBEYVILLE — In the 1950s a pregnant young woman, who had been hiding her condition, delivered her baby and then threw it over the side of the bridge. People say that if you turn your car off beneath the bridge it will not restart and then you will hear a crying baby.

NORTON — In an area known as Rogue's Hollow, local legend says that a young woman threw her baby off the bridge, simply because she didn't want it. Another version of the story claims that the woman was actually a witch who became pregnant by a married man. Locals descended on her home, carried off the baby, and threw it over the side. Some claim that the baby's cries are still heard, while others say you can actually see the woman throwing her baby into the water.

CABLE — This tale is a bit convoluted. It is said that a woman first threw her child off the bridge, then jumped over the side herself; both were killed by a passing train. Now people hear the crying baby, a screaming woman, and the approaching train.

EATON — This is another story of a frazzled woman who could no longer tolerate her baby's crying and so hurled the infant off the bridge. Now people claim to see something falling off the side of the bridge and to hear the wails of a baby.

LIMA — On Halloween night a woman driving over the bridge accidentally crashed her car, killing herself and her child. Visit the bridge on Halloween night and you will hear a baby rattle and a crying infant.

What's in a Name?
Crybaby Bridge
(continued)

TROY — In another accidental death story, a family was driving over the bridge when they had a wreck. The baby was presumed thrown into the creek below, but the body was never recovered. The baby still cries out to be found.

GRATIS — Apparently, many people have accidents driving over Ohio's bridges. In this story from the early 1900s, a group of young people returning home from a party crashed their car into the old covered Brubaker Bridge. All were killed and all the bodies recovered except for one, a boy. People parking on the bridge at night hear the boy's ghost knocking on the car windows.

MANSFIELD — Another Halloween night story, this one says that a mother named Mary Jane murdered her baby on the bridge. Some accounts say that the baby and mother were killed by persons unknown. Visitors to the bridge on Halloween can hear the sounds of the baby crying in the distance.

SALEM — Two ghosts are said to haunt the bridge on Egypt Road. It is said that a young couple was in the midst of an argument when the mother noticed that their little baby had crawled away. Too late, she spotted the child crawling near the edge of the bridge. The baby fell over the side and the mother was unable to save it. Today, you can hear the baby's cries and the bereaved mother's anguished screams.

SHELBY — It is said that an entire family was murdered on the bridge, but for whatever reason, only the ghostly cries of the baby are heard today.

CHAPTER 7

Oliver House
TOLEDO

IN THE MID-NINETEENTH CENTURY Toledo was a vibrant and bustling city. When the Oliver House opened its doors in 1859, it instantly became a fitting addition to this growing, energetic metropolis. Commissioned by Major William Oliver and designed by architect Isaiah Rogers, the first-class hotel was luxurious by the standards of its day. It featured private rooms with a view of the Maumee River, and each of the 171 rooms was appointed with its own fireplace, running water, and gaslights. Rosewood chairs, lace curtains, and a carved piano graced the public rooms of the elegant hotel. An omnibus ferried guests back and forth from the hotel to the train station.

Over the years other hotels sprang up in Toledo, offering competition to Oliver House, and the neighborhood surrounding the old hotel became more and more industrialized. By 1894 the once-fashionable hotel had been reduced to a common boardinghouse and, for a brief period, served as a hospital for veterans of the Spanish-American War. In 1919 the Riddle Co. purchased the building for the manufacturing of lighting fixtures and completely gutted the structure. Other industrial concerns occupied the building for several decades.

Today, Oliver House has been restored as much as possible to its antebellum days and is once again the site of social activity as several restaurants, bars, an art gallery, theater, and the Maumee Bay Brewing Co. have taken up residence in the building. There are even some condominiums in Oliver House.

It was a beautiful sunny May afternoon when my wife, Mary, and I pulled into the Oliver House parking lot. The building was an immense brick structure with "Oliver House" boldly spelled out in big white letters on one side of the building, just above the Maumee Bay Brewing Co.'s iconic great blue heron sign painted directly on the bricks.

There were no other cars in the lot—it was an odd time of day, right between lunch and dinner—but the building was open so we went inside. We walked up the gleaming white staircase to the brewery, all the while gawking at the framed prints, bar signs, and decorative plates hung cheek-by-jowl on every available wall surface. As we entered the pub we passed by gleaming copper brew vats standing behind the glass walls of the microbrewery.

There wasn't a soul in the pub, but there was a young guy behind the long bar who told us that the pub was open. The bartender's name was Anthony Fimognari and, while Mary sat at a table perusing the menu, I talked with him about the building and asked him directly if he had experienced the ghosts that were said to haunt the place.

Anthony told me that he had never seen a ghost there, but that he did have a brush with paranormal activity.

"I was behind the bar," he said, "working at one end. There were glasses standing on a shelf at the other end of the bar. All of a sudden, the glasses started to fall over."

"You were alone?" I asked.

"Yes, and on the opposite end of the bar from the glasses."

Anthony surprised me by saying that there was a photo of the Oliver House ghost. He reached under the bar and retrieved a piece of paper with the photocopied image of one of the creepiest looking men I had ever seen. The man seemed to have a dark beard and long hair with a receding hairline across a high, balding forehead. His eyes were indistinct, large black holes, like the empty eye sockets of a skull. He wore a white shirt—or was that a hospital gown?

Anthony said that the original picture was taken by a man who lived in one of the condos. He was coming down in the elevator alone, but he had the odd sensation that someone else was with him. He happened to have a camera with him, and when he stepped off the elevator he turned and took a picture. I was looking at the result.

"Who do you suppose it is?" I asked Anthony.

He said he didn't know but that the most common sighting in the building was that of a man in a blue military uniform, an apparition people at Oliver House call The Captain. Could The Captain have been one of the hospitalized veterans who died in the building when it was a hospital? And was that him in the photo?

Anthony called Ellie Barnett, the manager, to see if she would have some time to speak with me. Ellie said she could see me in a little while, so Mary and I decided to tuck into a late lunch of tasty pub food, which I washed down with a Buckeye Beer brewed on-site. The table cards in the pub read: *When you're dry . . . drink Buckeye.*

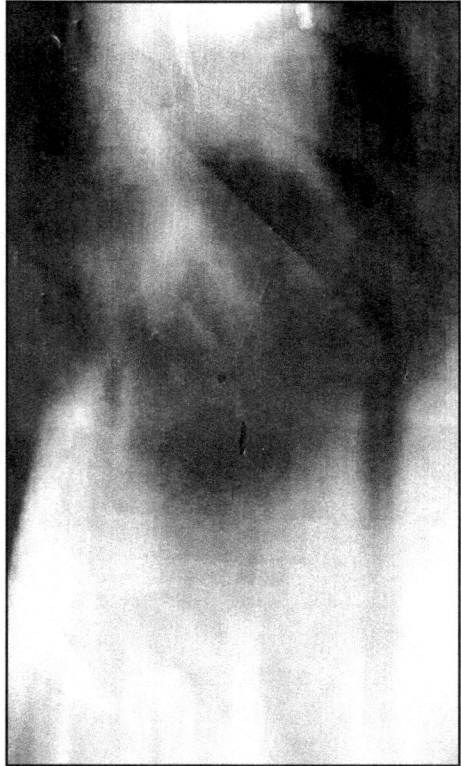

Oliver House ghost

After about twenty minutes Ellie came to our table and introduced herself. Ellie was convinced that there is at least one ghost in Oliver House, if not more.

"Once when I was all alone in the pub, I heard my name called three times," she said. "I also heard someone whistling another night. One of our distributors had been there that night and I thought it might be him, but it turned out I was alone; he had already left the building."

Ellie asked me if I would like a tour of the building. Would I? Of course!

The first room we entered was the ladies' restroom—we did knock first.

"We think there's a ghost that lives in this closet," Ellie said, indicating a closed door in the restroom. Patrons in the restroom often see and hear the closet doorknob violently rattling.

I opened the door. No ghost. I didn't expect there to be one since ghosts rarely appear on demand.

"One night a lady entered the restroom and found it empty. When she came out of the stall, there was a woman sitting in this chair," Ellie said, indicating a fancy little chair by the door. The woman in the chair had blonde hair, but other than that, she was in full skeletal form. When the lady ran out of the restroom, she was a nervous wreck, but we didn't find anything in the room.

"Another lady said that she saw a woman wearing a red hat in the restroom and that she wanted to go back to talk with her, but the lady in the hat was gone. No one else saw her anywhere in the building."

Ellie led me through the different dining areas and bars in the building. We stopped in a large semicircular ballroom that was originally the lobby of the hotel. Palladian windows in the curved wall threw warm rectangles of sunlight into the room. Patrons formerly entered from the street level and then came up a grand curving staircase to the lobby. Now, that area was filled with round tables draped in white tablecloths.

I looked around and noticed a paint-scarred metal door set into the wall. It had a heavy iron handle and the remains of a tumbler lock on it. A metal sign bolted on it read: *Herrin-Hall-Marvin Safe Co., Hamilton, O.* The door was flanked by a mini-refrigerator and a stove.

"That area used to be the front office," Ellie said, "and the safe was used for hotel receipts."

We continued our tour, crossing the courtyard and winding up in another pub called Mutz.

"The Captain has been seen right there, standing next to the bar," Ellie said. I walked over by the bar and saw an equipment closet, its door standing open. I took a few pictures there, but nothing out of the ordinary showed up.

When we returned to the Maumee Bay Brewing Co., we ran into Neal Kovacik, the general manager. Neal was a hale and hearty kind of guy wearing a white shirt and tie. He was interested in my investigation and related a few stories of his own.

Like Ellie, Neal had also heard someone whistling. That time it was in Petit Fours, a pastry shop in Oliver House.

"It was about six or seven in the morning," Neal said, "and I was alone. If you take a look outside, you'll see that this isn't the kind of neighborhood where a lot of people would be walking around outside that early in the morning. I don't know where the whistling came from."

Neal also told me about the time an employee working at Petit Fours came into work, saw a woman in white at the counter, and greeted her, thinking it was another employee named Molly. But when the first employee went into the work area of the store she found Molly there—dressed in black. When the two women came out to see the woman in white, she was gone. Neal pointed out that the event happened before the store was open for business.

Neal offered to show me the basement of the building, and the three of us made our way downstairs. It was dusty, and the floor of the basement was original hard-packed earth. There wasn't much to see down there—old boards, pipes, broken bricks—but there were several large drums of water that had been stored there since World War II. Neal also found cases of old French wine in a storeroom that hadn't been locked in many years.

There didn't seem to be any ghostly sightings associated with the basement, but that is probably the one place in the entire building that hadn't been altered since its original construction, so who knows? It might be worth further investigation.

Whether you're exploring the basement or the many food and drink areas, Oliver House is an intriguing place. If a man in blue offers to buy you a drink, take his picture quickly, before he disappears.

Spotlight On:
Toledo Ghost Hunters Society

Neither Harold St. John nor Butch Leon, cofounders of the Toledo Ghost Hunters Society (TOGHS), claim to have any special abilities in the occult or psychic realm. Instead, they rely upon "a serious, scientific approach to investigating paranormal activity through documentation, research, and the use of state-of-the-art electronic equipment." Founded in 2000, TOGHS considers its work a kind of public service and does not charge for its services.

In addition to St. John and Leon, the Toledo-based group includes Marie St ger, Becky McClenathen, and Michelle Maddux, with an additional ten associate members.

St. John says that the group's favorite haunted location is Athens, Ohio, a town widely regarded as perhaps the most haunted location in the state (see the chapter about The Ridges). "TOGHS has visited this sleepy community on several occasions," St. John says, "and has documented paranormal activity every time we visited."

For more information about the Toledo Ghost Hunters Society, see **toghs.org.**

Legendary Ghosts:
The Elmore Rider

Life is slow and predictable, if not downright boring, in the little town of Elmore, located about fifteen miles southeast of Toledo. But if life there is boring, death makes up for it because the sleepy town is home to the Elmore Rider.

It is said that a young soldier returning home at the end of World War I bought himself a brand new motorcycle and rode off to Elmore to visit the girl he had left behind. When he arrived at the girl's family farm, he discovered that the love of his life had become engaged to another man. Angry and hurt, the young soldier jumped on his motorcycle and roared off, his tears blinding him. Speeding into a curve in the road just before a bridge, he lost control of the bike and crashed into a ravine. Rescuers found the new motorcycle smashed into pieces and among the wreckage, the decapitated body of the young man.

Every March 21, the anniversary of the man's death, people standing on the bridge report seeing a light leaving the farm, entering the curve in the road, and then vanishing halfway across the bridge.

In 1968, a student at Bowling Green State University named Richard Gill decided to investigate the Elmore Rider sightings. Gill brought a friend along with him on the night of March 21. They had two cameras and a tape recorder with them. Following the ritual presumed to summon the ghost light, the pair parked their car on the far side of the bridge, flashed the lights three times, and honked the horn three times. Suddenly, the ghost light appeared, streaking out of the farm into the road and then disappearing upon the bridge.

Gill and his friend then ran a string across the bridge to see if the light was a solid object. Using their car, they summoned the light again. Once again, it flew up the road and onto the bridge before vanishing; the string remained intact.

Intrigued now, Gill's friend stood on the bridge while Gill remained on the far side. They called for the ghost light one more time. It appeared again, speeding up the road. When it disappeared, Gill found his badly bruised friend lying on the ground near the bridge. All he could remember was seeing a bright light hurtling toward him, then blackness.

In one final test, the friends parked the car on the side of the bridge closest to the farmhouse but pointed toward the other end of the bridge. They summoned the ghost light and began driving their car away from it as it approached from behind. The ghost light overtook the car, filling it with a flash of light, but then vanished into the darkness once more. The friend's cameras revealed only a vague light source, and the tape recorder picked up an unidentifiable high-pitched noise.

There are several similar headless-motorcyclist ghost stories circulating in the Midwest, leading one to believe that they are urban legends. Still, that possibility doesn't deter the many people who stand nocturnal watches on the bridges of Elmore, hoping to catch a glimpse of the Elmore Rider.

Ohio's Haunted Hotels

Ever think you might want to spend a night in a haunted hotel? Ohio is full of them. Here's a sampling of some of the spookiest:

Hilton Netherland Plaza – Cincinnati
This beautiful Art Deco hotel right in the heart of Cincinnati is home to the Lady in Green. The spirit of a woman who jumped out a window high atop the hotel after her husband was killed while working on the construction of the hotel, she is most often seen on the elevators wearing a fancy green dress.

Hotel Breakers – Sandusky
Located in Cedar Point Amusement Park, the hotel has been serving guests for more than 100 years. The hotel is haunted by the ghost of a woman named Mary who hanged herself in a room on the second floor.

Lafayette Hotel – Marietta
This venerable old hotel has survived frequent flooding of the Ohio River, so the ghosts who still reside here feel safe and secure. One of the most common ghosts is that of Mr. Hoag, a former hotel manager. The waitstaff in the hotel's restaurant still sees him working on his business papers there, long after closing.

The Old Stone House Bed & Breakfast – Marblehead
This bed-and-breakfast is supposedly haunted by the ghost of a little girl who fell out of a window and flew three floors to her death. Guests claim to hear flushing toilets on the third floor, and some have reported photographing orbs in haunted Room 11.

Rider's Inn – Painesville

The Rider's Inn was built in 1812 and has seen its share of travelers pass through. Suzanne Rider was the original landlady of the establishment, and apparently she has found it difficult to leave. At least one modern guest has reported a silent lady who looks like Suzanne admitting the guests to the inn late at night.

Siesta Motel – Norwich

In 1994, a man who had argued violently with his mother left their house and rented a room at the motel. He was awakened in the middle of the night by an intruder. A struggle ensued, and the man was killed. Guests and employees now hear slamming doors, crying and laughter, and whispered obscenities. Lights go on and off by themselves, and some guests have reported being struck by the unseen presence.

The Lofts Hotel – Columbus

The boutique hotel in Columbus's new Arena area began life in 1882 as the Carr Building and housed several different businesses until it became a hotel in 1998. Perhaps the Lady of the Lofts, a woman in Victorian clothing who haunts the hotel, was an employee in one of those businesses; we don't know. What we do know is that several people have glimpsed her from the corner of their eye in the stairwell and occasionally in the halls. Recently, a hotel security guard named Kevin heard a woman's horrific screaming on the second floor in the middle of the afternoon. For twenty minutes he frantically searched the area but never found an explanation for the screaming.

Ohio's Haunted Hotels
(continued)

The Lofts Hotel

Granville Inn – Granville

Right across the street from the haunted Buxton Inn—which has, among other ghosts, a ghost cat—the Granville Inn has its share of spooky visitors. Cold spots, odd tapping noises, and a piece of glass that *floated* from a hanging lamp to the floor are just some of the paranormal pranks reported here.

The Golden Lamb – Lebanon

One of America's venerable old inns, the Golden Lamb has seen scores of generals and presidents, writers and actors, sports figures and entertainers pass through its doors since it was established as a stage-coach stop in 1803. Many of these guests found the inn so comfortable that they simply decided to stay. Look for the ghosts of Senator Clement L. Vallandigham, who accidentally shot himself to death in what is today a dining room; or Ohio Supreme Court Justice Charles R. Sherman, father of Civil War general William T. Sherman; or the little daughter of Henry Clay, Eliza, who died from an illness at the inn.

Candlewood Suites – North Olmstead
The land upon which the hotel was built was formerly woodlands. The story behind the haunting says that a woman hanged herself in the woods and that her body was later discovered by construction workers. There are reports of cold spots in the hotel, and some employees say they have been touched by the ghost.

The Inn at Cedar Falls – Logan
The Inn, located in the scenic Hocking Hills area of southeastern Ohio, has several cabins and a main house that incorporates an original 1840 log cabin. Unsettling, eerie guitar music was first heard as the cabin was undergoing renovation in 1987 to become part of the inn. Beneath the birdsong you might hear Guitar Man still playing his haunting tunes.

Westgate Hotel – Sylvania
Maids working on the fourth floor of the hotel often see the apparition of a woman in old-time clothing; they call her "Isabella." The maids think she may be the ghost of Olive Ward, a local woman murdered by her husband in 1857. They also hear their names being called by unseen persons.

CHAPTER 8

Wood County Historical Center & Museum

BOWLING GREEN

IN THE NINETEENTH AND EARLY TWENTIETH CENTURIES, "poor farms" were common sights across the country. These charitable institutions were set up to care for the indigent, sick, mentally challenged, orphaned, homeless, and elderly members of society. Administrators believed that work was therapeutic, so the able-bodied residents of such places would be sent to work on the farms and in various other areas such as the laundry, kitchen, housekeeping, blacksmith shop, slaughterhouse, etc.

The Wood County Infirmary, as it was then known, was built along the banks of the Portage River in 1869. The center originally included a 200-acre farm, a variety of shops and barns, a small lunatic asylum, a pest house, powerhouse, ice ponds, and a cemetery called Sunset Acre, where as many as 500 inmates—many of them children—eventually found eternal repose.

Today, the graceful Victorian-style infirmary houses the Wood County Historical Center & Museum. Nearly all of the institution's buildings and the cemetery still remain on the grounds, which is now a fifty-acre public park. So much of the institution remains unchanged from its early days that it is easy to see why so many ghosts still reside there—for them, nothing has changed.

I visited the infirmary on a summer weekday and was pleasantly surprised to find that I was one of only a handful of visitors, which meant that I would have plenty of time to wander the grounds and to soak up whatever impressions I might receive there.

I parked my car in the visitors' lot, walked up the sidewalk across a manicured lawn, and entered the enclosed sun porch at the front of the building. There was a small group of people seated there, obviously engaged in a meeting. Tim Gaddie, the Volunteer Coordinator, detached himself from the group and came over to me. He welcomed me to the home, handed me a map and a brochure, and suggested the best itinerary for my self-guided tour.

The museum is housed in the two-story infirmary building and contains a varied and fascinating collection of exhibits and artifacts pertaining to Wood County and, of course, life at the poor farm. When the poor farm was active, residents were segregated by gender. Now, the rooms in the separate east and west wings house the many exhibits. There is simply too much to adequately cover here, but some of the more intriguing exhibits focus on the early Native American population of Wood County; military history; early medical devices and practices; a reproduction of the Reed General Store; Victorian furniture and artifacts, including a collection of Victorian undergarments cleverly called Victorian's Secret; and antique pianos and organs. Some of the rooms were made up to look as though they were still serving the inmates, such as the barber shop, kitchen, and laundry.

One particular area, the Infirmary Bedroom Exhibit, was grim and gave me a sense of sadness as I viewed the narrow iron hospital bed with its blue-and-white striped coverlet and the antique wooden wheelchair in the corner of the room. I discovered later that the room had actually served as the morgue rather than as a patient room, and I wondered if perhaps I had picked up on that.

Another interesting and wonderfully gruesome exhibit is the little jar containing three severed fingers of a murder victim. The jar is on display in the Government Exhibit; see if you can find it.

As I made my way through the exhibits, especially those dedicated to life at the poor farm, it became clear to me that life for the inmates was a mixed bag of blessings and hardships. While the administrators did their best to care for these unfortunates, such a mélange of ailments and personality types made it difficult for some patients to thrive. Others, especially those able-bodied and mentally sound folks, fared much better. It should be noted here that in the poor farm's 102-year history (it closed in 1971), one caring family ran the home for seventy years. Edward Farmer was superintendent for about twenty-six years, followed by his daughter, Annie (Farmer) Brandenberry.

While I wandered through the halls and many rooms of the infirmary, I was, for the most part, alone. With all the artifacts and photos surrounding me I had the sense that I had stepped back in time, that I was experiencing what it felt like to be a resident at the poor farm. Looking at the photos, gazing into the innocent yet somehow knowing eyes of a mentally challenged

Wood County Infirmary lunatic asylum room

resident, it felt almost as though he was speaking to me. My ears strained in the silent rooms for the sound of whispers and disembodied footsteps.

Yes, there were ghosts in this place, I was sure of that.

After my long tour of the museum I went back downstairs, where I met Mike McMaster, the center's educator. Mike was busy working on his computer, but when I told him about my book and my interest in the Wood County Infirmary, he was happy to reveal some of the ghost stories associated with the place.

I had already read an online account from a woman in 2006 named Bev Price who visited the museum with her daughter and son. They were in the Lunatic House, whose upstairs level was roped off to visitors. She wrote: *I started looking around in the cells where the displays are and my daughter went her own way in a different cell. A few minutes later I heard heavy footsteps upstairs. I called out to my daughter and said, "I told you not to go upstairs." She yelled back and told me she wasn't upstairs. In the meantime, the footsteps continued. A little upset with her, I said, "I can hear you up there!" She then told me she was right behind me . . . she was looking in the first cell in the front and I was in the back. The footsteps continued . . . we looked at each other and ran out!*

When I asked Mike about such occurrences, he told me that people often hear footsteps in the Lunatic House as well as in some of the other buildings. He also told me that various ghost-hunter groups had recorded EVPs (electronic voice phenomena) in some of the buildings, often calling *Help* or *Mommy*. One investigator recorded a spirit voice saying *I see the mirror* in a room decorated with two large mirrors.

"What else did these groups find?" I asked.

"I don't know for sure," Mike said. "I wasn't with them all the time. We don't allow them here anymore."

"Why is that? Did they cause problems?"

"Oh, no," he said, "not at all. It's just that we don't have the manpower to have someone here all night with them. But it's not like we don't already have a lot of ghost stories about the place.

"My own daughter was here once," Mike continued, "complaining about the other children in one of the rooms who wouldn't play with her. There was no one else here at the time besides me and her."

It seemed that children in particular were witnesses to the ghosts. Mike told me about the little girl who looked up at the top of the stairs in the infirmary and said that she saw a man up there with a Bible who was going to escape. How did this little girl even understand the concept of escaping from such a place unless she was hearing the ghost speak to her? No one else saw the man.

Another time, a little boy about eight years old was at the poor farm with a church group. He came inside the infirmary and walked around for a little while. He went upstairs and when he came back down he noticed a photo of an old woman hanging on the wall. He pointed to it and said, "That's the lady I saw upstairs." The woman in the photo, of course, had long since shuffled off this mortal coil, and there was no one else upstairs when the boy was up there. Mike said he did not doubt the boy's story. He described the boy as "well groomed and articulate, a church kid."

Mike also told me about the pharmacist who lived nearby who used to make trips out to the farm to dispense prescriptions to the inmates.

"After so many trips out here, he started to recognize the residents on sight," Mike said. "One night he came out here and saw an old woman in her pajamas standing in the hall. He didn't recognize her and before he could say anything to her, she disappeared before his eyes.

"But that wasn't the only apparition seen here," Mike said. "One of our former employees saw a figure on the stairs going down to the basement."

Mike also said that a film production company had come out to the poor farm to make a documentary about it, including the ghost stories. They apparently got more than they bargained for, because one of the security lights that are constantly turned on began to flash on and off by itself, something it had never done before.

After my talk with Mike, I went outside and walked over to Sunset Acre, the poor farm cemetery. Here, in a neatly kept lot, simple headstones are lined up, denoting the final resting place of those poor souls who died while living at the farm.

Wood County Infirmary interior

Like so many other institutional cemeteries, especially those located at old mental asylums, the stones were blank except for a number. No names, no birth dates, no death dates. Nothing at all to connect them with those left behind. I understand that this anonymity is an effort to spare surviving family members embarrassment over the fact that one of their own died under such circumstances, but there is an ineffable sadness associated with such stones, and I thought of the inscription upon the Tomb of the Unknown Soldier at Arlington National Cemetery: *Known only to God.* I could not help but wonder if perhaps some of the ghosts were reaching out to the living, begging the living to recognize them as their own, to see them once again.

We may never know why the ghosts of Wood County Infirmary linger still in its silent halls; we may never know their identities. But this much we do know; there are many sightings of ghosts at this place and, no doubt, many more yet to come. Perhaps you will be lucky enough to experience one for yourself.

CHAPTER 9

Thomas Edison Birthplace
MILAN

ON A WET AND WINDY SATURDAY AFTERNOON—
gray clouds scudding overhead and red maple leaves spattered
on the street like blood—my wife, Mary, and I visited the little
house in Milan where Thomas Alva Edison was born on February 11, 1847.

There was another couple on the tour with us and a skinny
guy with a worried expression behind oversized glasses and a
scrawny neck accented by a large Adam's apple. He looked like
a chicken with a goiter, if chickens wore cowboy hats, as did this
man. While our elderly tour guide told us about the house, the
Cowboy kept up a stream of unfunny comments. Luckily, our
elderly tour guide—who looked something like Edison himself,

with his white hair plastered across his head—was hard of hearing (as was Edison) and so remained unfazed by the Cowboy's inane remarks.

Sometimes, this is the way things go when one is hunting ghosts.

To be truthful, I had no idea if the Edison house was haunted or not. I had just given a presentation about ghosts at the Milan-Berlin Public Library, and my wife and I decided to take a mini-vacation in the historic little town, booking a room at the Angel Welcome Bed & Breakfast on Front Street. A history buff, I had a great time walking around the town and by a stroke of dumb luck—one could call it good luck—discovered the Edison house only a few blocks from Angel Welcome.

Sometimes, this is also the way things go when one is hunting ghosts.

The house was a neat little brick cottage, surrounded by a white picket fence. Four windows flanked by black shutters lined the front of the house, a single white door situated in the center of them. We joined the group and entered the house through a side door.

Our tour guide stood beside a wooden rocking chair in the sitting room and gave us an overview of Edison's life, pointing out family paintings and photographs in the room as he spoke. Edison's ancestors had been prominent Loyalists in New Jersey at the time of the American Revolution and fled to Nova Scotia, Canada. They lived in that country for some time until Edison's father, Samuel, became embroiled in a Canadian political struggle that forced him to escape to the United States in the mid-nineteenth century, settling in Ohio, where Thomas was born. The tiny room in which he entered the world was just off the sitting room.

Our guide led us up a narrow and steep staircase to the two tiny bedrooms upstairs, used by Thomas's sisters and his

Thomas Edison

parents. I'm not an exceptionally tall guy, but my head nearly touched the low ceilings in those rooms; somehow, the Cowboy managed to keep his hat on.

So far, the rooms had been sparsely furnished and, despite the photos on display, I did not feel Edison's presence in the house. Perhaps I should not have been surprised since he only lived there a few years before his family moved to Port Huron, Michigan, in 1854.

Our guide, who, I swear, was beginning to look more and more like the photos of Edison as the tour continued, led us back down the stairs to a small room off the parlor. The walls were covered with photos of Edison and his various laboratories, especially the one in New Jersey that earned him the nickname "The Wizard of Menlo Park." Glass display cases held some of his many inventions; Edison held 1,093 U.S. patents and is credited with such inventions as the phonograph, the stock ticker, the motion picture camera, and, of course, the first long-lasting and practical lightbulb.

Down one more flight of stairs to the unremarkable kitchen located in the walk-out basement. It was an old-fashioned kitchen filled with old-fashioned apparatus. The tour concluded there as our guide led us out through the rear door of the house.

I let the Cowboy find his horse and waited for the other couple to leave before asking the guide if the house was haunted. Why not, I thought, you never know. He finished locking the door and turned to me with a smile, the first one I had seen on him all day.

"Well," he said, seemingly unfazed by my question, "we do think we might have a ghost in the house, maybe a few."

"Really?" I was surprised that my random question had hit pay dirt. "What can you tell me about them?"

He started to walk around to the front of the house and I went with him, notebook in hand.

"In later life, Thomas Edison bought this house, his childhood home, although he did not live in it. Ironically, the house was still being illuminated by candles when he made his last visit to the house in 1923. A cousin of Edison's mother lived in the house as something of a caretaker; we think she might still be here."

"People have seen her?" I asked.

"They've heard her laughing in the parlor, or heard a door closing. Other people have seen the rocking chair by the side door begin to rock on its own, with no one near it."

We had walked around the house and up the hill to the front. I shook hands with our guide and thanked him for all the great information he had given us, paranormal and otherwise. That's when he told me that our tour would be its last since the Edison House, like so many other historical sites, was facing economic hardships and was letting go its docents; the house would only be open on special occasions until more funds were available.

Mary and I went inside the house next door, which was where he had purchased our tickets for the tour. A young man who had not been there earlier sat at the desk. His name was Shane Wolfkill, and he told us that he was also a tour guide at the house. I asked him if he knew of any ghost stories related to the house.

"Oh, sure," he said, "there are lots. Sometimes people will hear whispering in their ear when no one is around, and one visitor even heard a voice say out loud, 'Get out!' One thing that's really weird is that people will get the feeling that there is someone watching them. hanging around close to them, besides the other people on the tour, but when they look around, there is no one else there."

"Is it only one ghost?"

"Two, we think." Shane replied. "There's the woman, who we think is an Edison cousin; she's in the parlor. But then there's another ghost in the kitchen and that one we think is a man."

"Do you know who that one may be?" I asked.

He shook his head. "No, but most people that have sensed him there feel that it is not Thomas Edison."

I suppose that makes sense, since Edison spent so little of his life in the house, and that as a young boy. But we should remember that one of the inventions Edison was working on when he died was a machine that would allow the living to speak with the dead. Although he never completed his machine—nor has anyone else who has tried—it is clear that he had some interest in the spirit world and life after death. Are we really sure that The Wizard of Menlo Park hasn't yet found a way to speak to us who still live? Are we really sure that he is not there in his boyhood home just waiting to say 'hello'?

Central

Columbus
Central Ohio Fire Museum & Learning Center
Kelton House
Thurber House

Lucas
Malabar Farm

Mansfield
Ohio State Reformatory

CHAPTER 10

Kelton House
COLUMBUS

THERE ARE SO MANY GHOST STORIES associated
with the Kelton House in Columbus that the volunteer staff
there has put them down in writing, a collection of stories that
span the last thirty years, if not longer.

I had first heard about Kelton House in 2003 as I was writing *Ghosthunting Ohio*. Nellie, a supervisor at the house, contacted me to tell me about the ghosts, but for a host of reasons I
was unable to visit there before the book was published. Nellie
and I stayed in touch and I vowed to rectify the situation with
my next book about Ohio ghosts, so in 2009 I finally visited
Kelton House.

Built by Fernando and Sophia Kelton in the mid-nineteenth century, the beautiful two-story brick home sits on a shaded street in a historic section of Columbus. Two floor-to-ceiling windows flank the impressive front door; three windows are arranged across the façade of the second floor, the middle one accented by a graceful wrought iron balcony.

Although we had corresponded for almost six years, Nellie and I had never met, so it was nice to finally meet her in person as she greeted me at the front door. She wore a red blouse beneath a black blazer and red and black house slippers; she wore her red hair pulled back and tied. Frankly, I was a bit taken back by her scarlet fashion sense until she explained to me that it was a way of memorializing the last Kelton who lived in the house.

Grace Kelton, Nellie explained, had studied design and had assisted Jacqueline Kennedy when the First Lady redecorated the White House. Grace was well known in Columbus and loved the color red. Right up until her death in 1975 at the age of ninety-four, Grace was renowned for her red high heels, dyed-red hair, red lipstick, and red Cadillac.

"Maybe my attire is a way of connecting with Grace," Nellie said.

"Connecting?" I asked. "Is she still here?"

"We feel her presence often, but she's only one of several ghosts in the house."

I wanted to talk more with Nellie, but just then a young couple came in who wanted to talk with her about renting the house for their upcoming wedding. I was lucky, though, as one of the volunteers, decked out in a period hoopskirt, was about to begin a tour of the house.

Subha Lembach took us from room to room, each of them richly appointed in period furnishings. Apparently, ghosts are as commonplace in the house as the furniture, and Subha was not shy about sharing some of their stories.

She said that the house had a rich history, including its days as a stop on the Underground Railroad, the nineteenth-century network of safe houses that allowed runaway slaves to escape to freedom in the North, or further to Canada; Ohio was full of such houses. The Keltons aided countless numbers of runaway slaves, hiding them in the house's 300-barrel cistern or in the servants' quarters until they could be safely moved on.

That history might explain at least one apparition in the house, experienced by a napping docent. The volunteer was taking a nap during a slow time at the house. She awoke suddenly to see a "black man" leaning over her, peering at her. A second later, he disappeared.

Subha led us into the dining room where a long table, set with elegant dinnerware, sat beneath a crystal chandelier. A fireplace stood at one end of the room. She directed our attention to an antique sideboard against the wall. Silver serving pieces were arranged upon it. Above the sideboard hung an oval painting of Sophia Kelton. Careful to stand to one side of it, she told us that once when she was giving a tour she made the mistake of standing in front of the sideboard.

"One of the doors," Subha said, pointing them out to us, "flew open with force and hit me from behind. I closed it and it burst open again, hitting me. It did that three times before it stopped."

She went to the doors and demonstrated how securely closed they were; it would not be easy for them to simply open on their own. Subha pointed to the portrait of Sophia. "I think she was trying to tell me I was blocking the visitors' view of her portrait," she said with a laugh.

Our group proceeded up to the second floor. An old Regina-phone stood in the center hall before the balconied window at the front of the house. The instrument was essentially a huge music box. The cabinet stood about four feet high. Inside, a large metal disk punctuated with little spikes was operated by a hand crank on the side of the cabinet. Subha showed us how it worked.

"It takes some strength to turn the crank," she said. After a few turns, she released the crank and loud, melodious music filled the house. When the music stopped, Subha let me try the crank; it was not easy to turn.

"That's why we can't understand how the music will suddenly play all by itself, when no one is there," she said.

Lying on the floor by the Reginaphone was a child's toy crib. Two dolls lay inside it. One day a visitor to the house saw a little girl kneeling on the floor, playing with the dolls. The man knew that the dolls were probably antiques, so he said something to the girl about being careful with them. She turned around and the man saw that she had no eyes. He left the house in a hurry. Later, a medium working in the house also sensed the presence of the eyeless little girl.

When Subha completed the tour, I wandered out into the lush gardens at the rear of the house. Brick walks bordered by hedges, set every now and then with benches, surrounded the gardens. At the rear a white pergola provided a peaceful setting for reflection, or simply relaxing. It was easy to see why so many brides would be interested in renting the house for their receptions. As I sat on a bench, taking in the ambience—and perhaps, the paranormal energy of the place—I spied Nellie leading prospective clients through the gardens.

After meditating for a while in the gardens, I returned to the house, where I caught up with Nellie. She was glad to hear that I had taken the house tour, but she had stories of her own to add to those of Subha.

Nellie led me into a small sitting room at the front of the house. She told me that a guest at a wedding reception there had glanced into the room and saw several Civil War soldiers sitting there. She also told me that one time a woman touring the house had seen a young man wearing a Union army uniform sitting in the room, smoking.

"The woman told one of our volunteers that she thought it was great that we had volunteers in the house wearing Civil War uniforms. Very authentic, she thought, except the problem was that we didn't have any volunteers in the house wearing uniforms, or anywhere else for that matter," Nellie said.

Later, the woman went down into the basement where there is now a display about the history of the Kelton family and the house. As she viewed the exhibit, she was startled to see an old photo that matched perfectly the man she had seen in the sitting room upstairs.

"The man she identified," Nellie said, "was Oscar Kelton, a son of Fernando and Sophia, who served in the Union army and was killed at the battle of Bryce's Crossroads in 1864."

Nellie has had several encounters with the paranormal at Kelton House. She was fortunate to have captured an EVP (electronic voice phenomena) on her recorder of a woman's loud scream and giggling children. Once, when she was giving a tour, the lights went out in the bedroom where both Fernando and Sophia had died. Nellie said something aloud about needing light and, suddenly, the lights came back on. Nellie has seen a figure that she described as a "silhouette" waving its arms and another peeking from behind a door; some of the kitchen staff has seen Sophia Kelton on the staircase looking down at them.

Nellie said that several years ago, when the house was being restored, workers would leave their tools and equipment scattered around the house. In the middle of the night the security alarm in the house would go off, and when the police arrived they would find all the material placed in neat piles and any furniture that the workers had moved returned to its proper place. Obviously, the ghost of Grace Kelton is still very much interested in design and good taste.

Nellie took me upstairs, past the second floor, to a small landing on the third floor where there was nothing but a door that led to the attic. Nellie told me that it was believed that Arthur Kelton, the black sheep of the family, suffered from dementia and was kept in the attic, which is now where the volunteers change into their costumes. Nellie said that people feel uncomfortable up there and that sometimes, when the door is opened, a whoosh of cold air sweeps past them. She also said that a "fortune teller" who was in the attic was scared away by what she called a "scary ghost." Could that be Arthur Kelton? I was hoping to spend some time up there, but Arthur had other ideas. The door was locked and Nellie was unable to unlock it.

There have been several psychics, mediums, and ghosthunting groups who have visited Kelton House over the years, and many of them have had paranormal experiences. One medium connected with the spirit of a woman dressed in blue, who she called Belle. Had she connected with the same ghost in blue that a visitor had mistaken for a volunteer? Is that ghost Isabelle Coit Kelton, a daughter-in-law of Fernando and Sophia?

There are far too many ghost stories about the Kelton House to mention them all here. The best thing you can do is visit the house for yourself. And wear red . . . Grace may be watching.

Spotlight On:
Ohio's Confederate Ghosts

Just across the Ohio River, marking the state's southern border, lies Kentucky, a state that was neither Confederate nor Union during the Civil War but was hotly contested by both sides. As might be expected, there were a fair number of Confederate sympathizers living in southern Ohio, and in 1863 Confederate Gen. John Hunt Morgan led his Rangers in a protracted raid through the state, coming to within a day's ride of Lake Erie, until they were captured near Liverpool, Ohio. It was the deepest penetration into the North made by any Confederate unit during the war.

Morgan and his officers were imprisoned in the Ohio Penitentiary in Columbus, from which they escaped only a few months later, eventually making their way back to the Confederacy. Morgan's captured enlisted men, however, were confined in Columbus at a Union training and prisoner-of-war camp that received thousands of Confederate soldiers during the war.

Camp Chase's facilities may have been better than most, but 2,260 Confederate soldiers died there from disease and malnutrition,

Spotlight On:
Ohio's Confederate Ghosts
(continued)

which may explain why the cemetery—all that today remains of Camp Chase—is haunted. The most famous ghost, though, is not a soldier but that of a mysterious, veiled Lady in Grey who, over many years, has been seen visiting the grave of Private Benjamin F. Allen of the 50th Tennessee. No one knows the identity of this mourning ghost. Is she Allen's fiancée? Wife? Mother or sister? It has been some time since the Lady in Grey was last seen at Camp Chase. Perhaps she has finally been reunited with her beloved Benjamin.

Another large prisoner-of-war camp was located on Johnson's Island, overlooking Sandusky Bay. At least 10,000 Confederate prisoners, most of them officers, were processed into the camp's stockade during the forty months it was in operation.

There are at least 206 soldiers buried in the camp's cemetery, although recent studies indicate that there may be many more bodies buried in unmarked graves; Sherri Brake, a noted regional ghosthunter and descendant of Confederate General "Stonewall" Jackson, has discovered the final resting place of some of these soldiers using dowsing rods.

Today, shadowy figures are seen moving through the cemetery, while some people also report hearing voices near the old camp. One of the most unusual ghost stories from the camp concerns Italian immigrants who were working in the now-defunct quarry on Johnson's Island. It's not uncommon for workmen to sing while they work, but it was strange to hear these Italian men singing "Dixie" together, especially since most of them spoke no English. Where had they learned that great old Southern song? Is it possible, as some think, that they had heard it being sung by the Confederate ghosts who roam the nearby cemetery?

These cemeteries give new meaning to the slogan *The South shall rise again* and are certainly worth visiting when you're in the area.

CHAPTER 11

Thurber House
COLUMBUS

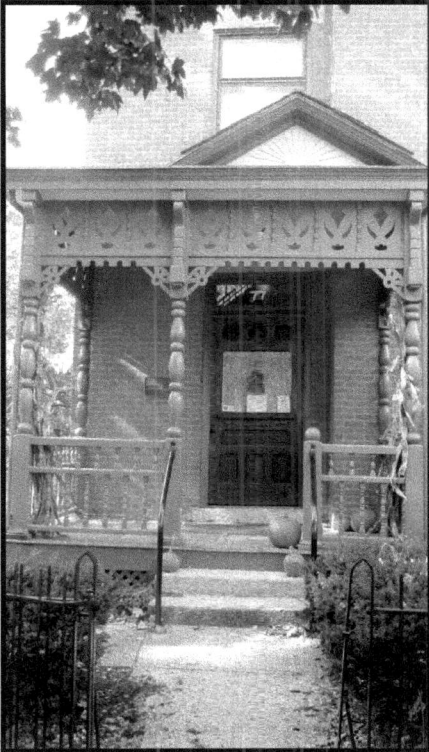

JAMES THURBER (1894–1961) was one of America's most famous humorists and is one of this writer's favorites. A native Buckeye, Thurber was born in Columbus and graduated from Ohio State University before moving to New York City in 1925, where he found fame writing for *The New Yorker* magazine.

While a student at Ohio State, Thurber's family rented a house at 77 Jefferson Street, a house that later figured in some of his short stories, most notably "The Night the Ghost Got In." What makes this story so fascinating is that, while some of the details may be embellished, it is a true story.

Thurber relates that he was taking a shower upstairs one evening when he heard some noises from the dining room below. His father and one of his brothers were away at Indianapolis at the time and his other brother and mother were upstairs, his grandfather in the guest room in the attic. So, who was downstairs? Wrapping a towel around him, he stepped out into the hall where his brother was also listening to the noise from below. The two boys silently crept to the head of the stairs.

In the story, Thurber writes that what they heard was ". . . the footsteps of a man walking rapidly around the dining room table downstairs . . . 'There's something down there!' I said. Instantly the steps began again, circled the dining room table like a man running, and started up the stairs toward us, heavily, two at a time. The lights still shone palely down the stairs; we saw nothing coming, we only heard the steps."

The boys ran into their bedrooms and slammed the doors just as the footsteps would have reached them. Their mother, alarmed by all the commotion, was certain burglars had entered the house. According to the story, she threw a shoe through the window of their neighbor Bedwell's house (the houses were very close to each other) in order to get him to call the police. Thurber writes, "Bedwell at first thought that she meant there were burglars in his house, but finally quieted down and called the police for us over an extension phone by his bed. After he had disappeared from the window, Mother suddenly made as if to throw another shoe, not because there was further need of it but, as she later explained, the thrill of heaving a shoe through a window glass had enormously taken her fancy. I prevented her."

James Thurber

Chaos breaks out in the story as the police arrive. They give the towel-clad Thurber a funny look and rush upstairs to the attic where Thurber's grandfather, a Civil War veteran, was still sleeping soundly through all the mayhem. Grandpa had a gun, and he knew how to use it. Suddenly roused from his slumber by the police, whom he mistakes for Union army deserters, he fires a shot and wings one in the shoulder, forcing them to beat a hasty retreat downstairs. How much of this last part is true and how much is fiction remains a mystery but, in any case, it makes a great story.

This episode haunted Thurber his whole life. Many years later he was asked why he did not reveal the actual location of the house in his story. His reply was, "I definitely changed the address of the house for the simple reason there was a ghost in the house." He did not want to prevent future renters from occupying the house.

Today, the house at 77 Jefferson Street is both a memorial to Thurber and a literary center. Many famous writers, whose numerous photos adorn the stairway and hall of the house, have lectured or read from their works at Thurber House, and each year the house hosts writers-in-residence, who are accommodated in the attic, formerly Grandpa's bedroom, now a renovated and comfortable suite of rooms.

But the house remains haunted.

It was October when I visited Thurber House, and the porch was decorated with pumpkins and corn shocks. The house looks small from outside; one large window with beautiful scrollwork etching beside a single door located on the little Victorian gingerbread porch. I was greeted at the house by Anne Touvell, manager of adult literary programs, and Patricia Shannon, director of children's programming. They took me on a tour of the three floors of the house, where I got to see the true dimension of the large house. The downstairs remains essentially as it was in Thurber's day, the beautifully appointed parlor looking as though it were ready to welcome guests at any time. The notorious table still remains in the center of the dining room, but the room itself is now a gift shop.

I walked up the rear stairs from the dining room to the bedrooms—the same stairs upon which the ghost ascended—pausing to admire the framed photos of famous authors hanging there. On the second floor is Thurber's small and sparsely furnished bedroom with his old Underwood typewriter—the machine he used at *The New Yorker*—resting on a small table. The door to the closet in that room has been removed, revealing the signatures of dozens of authors who had been guests in Thurber's room.

Back downstairs Anne told me that Jason and Grant, the stars of TV's *Ghost Hunters*, had come to the house to conduct an investigation; the segment titled "It's Time to Get Touched" aired only a few days before my visit, although I did not know about it until Anne told me.

"What did they find?" I asked.

Anne pointed to a small mantel clock. "At one point, the glass case swung open all by itself. There's a latch on it, see?" she said, pointing out the little metal latch. "That latch was closed. We never touched it."

It turns out that the TV guys had the clock checked by an expert who verified that the latch was in working order and shouldn't have opened.

"They were a little confused, though," Anne said. "When you watch the video you see them calling James, as if he was the ghost that was here. He's not. He experienced the ghost himself, so how could it be him?"

"If the ghost is not Thurber, then who is it?"

"We don't know for sure," Anne said, "but the land on which this house stands, actually the whole street, was once the site of the Ohio Lunatic Asylum. There was a huge fire there in which several women died. That might have something to do with it."

I agreed with her. Coincidentally, the ghostly event described by Thurber occurred exactly forty-seven years to the day after that tragic fire.

Over the years many guests and writers-in-residence have heard the same footsteps downstairs in the former dining room or racing up the stairs. When I had a chance to view the *Ghost Hunters* program. I was surprised by the way in which Jason and Grant dismissed the sounds. Grant stood at the top of the stairs while Jason stomped around in the dining room and then ran to the front door as though he were a burglar fleeing the house after being surprised by the young Thurber. Grant said that Jason's retreating footsteps could easily sound like they were coming up the stairs instead. While I would admit to that possibility, neither of the men ran up the stairs—heavily and two steps at a time as Thurber reported—to see what *that* would sound like. I'm sure there would be a big difference, one that a boy who lived in the house for four years would easily recognize. In short, I still believe Thurber.

Anne told me about some of the experiences that Terri and Sheila, the Thurber House housekeepers, had experienced. One time the women were working on the first floor. They had pulled the chairs away from the wall in the middle room so that they could vacuum the rugs. When they finished, they put the chairs back in their proper places and left the room. When they came by later, they found that all the chairs had been pulled out again.

Terri was so unnerved by paranormal events in the house that she would never work there alone. A friend accompanied her to the house on one of her visits. As they were leaving the house, Terri remembered that she had left a light on in one of the rooms. Her friend joked that she should "just let the ghost get it." At that moment the china cabinet in the alcove off the middle room began to shake, as though someone were shaking it, rattling the glasses and dishes inside.

Another time Terri was in the house with her son and two nieces. She finished cleaning downstairs, and the whole group went up to the second floor. When they got there the piano on the first floor began playing by itself. At the same time, the computer in Anne Touvell's office on the second floor started to turn off and on of its own accord.

Sheila once felt a cold rush of air sweep by her on the stairs leading up to the third floor.

A former resident of the house named Esther Reich—she lived there from 1936 until 1942—reported often hearing footsteps running up the rear stairs. Perhaps even more unnerving, Esther awoke one night to see the figure of a man hunched over in the rocking chair, his elbow on his knee; in an instant, he vanished.

Writers, especially fiction writers, may be prone to flights of fantasy, but more than one writer-in-residence has had encounters of a paranormal, if not fantastical, nature at Thurber House. Nearly all the residents have heard the phantom footsteps on the stairs, and several of them have seen the shadowy figure of a man. One female writer saw the shadow of a stooped, hefty man wearing a raincoat with the collar turned up (only a writer would note such details!) walk by the windows of the attic apartment, although she was alone in the house at the time.

Lisa Yee was a writer-in-residence at Thurber House for a month. Once, when looking at a framed picture, she saw a man reflected in the glass. She quickly turned around to find no one there.

Lisa also said that, while working in the attic apartment, her computer would sometimes go haywire. She would write out a story on the computer at night and awaken to find that her words had been changed. Either she was a sleepwalking writer, or she had run into a cantankerous editor-ghost.

The day that her residency ended, Lisa was walking downstairs early in the morning. The stairs were dark, and she suddenly felt the air around her become thick, as though she were walking through JELL-O. She thought that she had walked through a spiderweb but, when she turned on the lights, there was nothing there. (I know what she felt, having had the exact same thing happen to me at the Collingwood Art Center in Toledo, a place haunted by something the artists there called Shadowman.)

The mission of Thurber House is, in part, "to celebrate the written word for the education and entertainment of the broadest possible audience . . ." Even though the identities of the ghosts at Thurber House remain a mystery, it's nice to know that their very presence may inspire writers to create some new ghostly and entertaining stories.

Academic Ghosts

It seems that many ghosts are roaming the hallowed halls of Ohio's colleges and universities, no doubt majoring in Metaphysics or Paranormal Studies. Here's a sampling of some of the more notable academic hauntings:

Bowling Green State University (Bowling Green) – The university is home to more than one ghost. The most famous is Alice, who haunts the university's theater. It is unclear how she died; some stories say she was an actress on stage and was killed when something fell from the catwalks above, while another say that she was killed in a car crash. In any case, she haunts the theater, and tradition holds that the stage manager must formally invite her to every upcoming performance or she will wreak havoc on the production, knocking things over, playing with the lights and sound equipment, and generally making a nuisance of herself. Several people have seen Alice and describe her as a young woman with long hair, dressed in 1920s-style clothing.

The Chi Omega sorority house is still home to Amanda, a woman who rushed the sorority but was killed by a train on the very night she was to be made a sister. Undeterred by something as trivial as death Amanda remains an active sister, knocking items off walls, locking and unlocking doors, stealing objects and depositing them in a closet, and turning lights off and on.

Kenyon College (Gambier) – The oldest private college in Ohio, prestigious Kenyon College may be one of the most haunted as well. Norton Hall is haunted by the ghost of a student who committed suicide, while Manning Hall is haunted by the ghost of a female student who arrived at the campus but died before she was able to take any classes. In frustration, she moves the furniture and rearranges the personal belongings of students in her former dormitory. Lewis Hall is haunted by yet another suicide, a student who hanged himself in the attic. Students hear knocking on their doors only to find no one on the other side, toilets flush, and lights go on and off by themselves.

The college's Bolton Dance Studio is located in a building that once housed the swimming pool. Legend has it that a high-diver hit his head on the ceiling and drowned when he fell into the pool. Although the pool is long gone, people still hear the sounds of someone swimming and also struggling in the water, as if drowning. They hear voices and watery footprints appear on the floor, apparently walking through walls. The Wertheimer Fieldhouse is also haunted by an athletic ghost that runs laps on the track and opens and closes doors.

Caples Hall has the ghost of a jilted boyfriend who likes to touch coeds and sometimes moves their dressers in front of their doors, while the ghost of Stuart Pierson haunts Delta Kappa Epsilon fraternity house. Pierson was pledging the fraternity in 1905 when he died trying to cross a train trestle. Poor Pierson's face is seen peering through the window, and he is heard walking around in his room each year on the anniversary of his death.

In 1949 a building known as Old Kenyon burned to the ground, killing nine men. The building was reconstructed—several inches higher than the original building—and the ghosts of these men are seen from the knees up walking down the hall, as if they were walking on the previous lower floors.

As if these hauntings weren't bad enough, it is said that the college gates are situated over a mouth to Hell, which may explain the devilish exams inflicted upon Kenyon students.

Academic Ghosts
(continued)

Miami University (Oxford) — One of the oldest public universities in Ohio, Miami University has at least two notable ghosts roaming its halls. The ghost of Judge Elam Fisher haunts Fisher Hall (named for him) and the surrounding grounds. He is believed to be the cause of items disappearing from the residents' dormitory rooms.

But the most mysterious disappearing act occurred in 1953 when sophomore Richard Tammen vanished from his dorm room in Fisher Hall without a trace. On the evening of April 19, Tammen was studying a psychology text in his dorm room. When his roommate returned to their room at 10:30 he found the lights on and Tammen's book lying facedown on the desk. Although Tammen was not there, the roommate did not think anything was amiss because Tammen sometimes spent the night at his fraternity house. But when Tammen didn't return the following day the authorities were called. They conducted a search but the student never turned up, nor was any evidence uncovered that pointed toward a possible explanation of his fate; he had simply vanished into thin air. When the old Fisher Hall was razed in 1978, police searched the rubble for clues, but nothing turned up. Fifty-eight years later Tammen's disappearance remains a mystery. While his person may have vanished, some people think Tammen's spirit is still there, lingering at the site of Fisher Hall; they have the vague feelings of an unseen presence with them.

Ohio University (Athens) — Athens may be Ohio's most haunted town and the venerable old Ohio University, founded in 1804, contributes its share of ghosts. One of the most haunted buildings on the campus is the former Athens Lunatic Asylum, now nicknamed "The Ridges." Once the residence of Billy Milligan, the infamous rapist with multiple personality disorder, the building is now haunted by various apparitions that appear to art instructors who maintain private studios in the building. The Ohio Exploration Society once conducted an investigation in the building and recorded an EVP (electronic voice phenomena) of a ghostly voice whispering, *Get us out of here*

Wilson Hall, a dormitory, is said to be located at the center of a pentagram made up of five local cemeteries, and so is supposedly paranormally active. While the cemeteries may in fact form a pentagram, there are so many small cemeteries in the Athens area that one could create any geometric shape one wanted.

The Zeta Tau Alpha house was once a stop on the Underground Railroad. The story goes that a runaway slave named Nicodemus sought refuge there but was discovered and killed by slave-catchers. Nicodemus remains there and enjoys fondling the sorority sisters.

Sinclair Community College (Dayton) — Located in downtown Dayton, Sinclair Community College was built on the ground where the city's public gallows once stood. That macabre location may be the explanation for the ghosts that haunt the college. People in Blair Hall feel invisible hands tugging at them and hear disembodied voices laughing and the sounds of invisible footsteps. Elevators work on their own, and doors slam shut.

A security guard on duty one night saw his boss walking down the hall toward him. That would be no surprise had the boss not died the week before.

A ghost called Mr. Joshua is seen in Building 13, the former site of United Color Press. It is believed that he is the ghost of a man who was killed when his arm was caught in the press. Mr. Joshua is described as an older white-haired man wearing jeans and a white shirt. He is seen in the hallways and walking through walls.

CHAPTER 12

Central Ohio Fire Museum & Learning Center
COLUMBUS

THE CENTRAL OHIO FIRE MUSEUM & LEARN-
ING CENTER is housed in a grand old fire station, replete
with beautiful architectural details and an imposing bell tower.
Opened in 1908 as No. 16 Engine House, the station was the
last one in the Columbus area to use horse-drawn firefighting equipment; the old horse stalls are still in the rear of the
building. The Engine House served the residents of Columbus
up until 1982, at which point it was slated for demolition. But
through the efforts of many firefighters who volunteered their
time and money, as well as the establishment of a nonprofit
organization to manage the center, the elegant firehouse was
saved for posterity. The firefighters restored the exterior to its

1908 appearance, renovated the first floor, and designed and built all of the displays. As a result of their efforts the building was added to the National Register of Historic Places. More than 1,500 area firefighters continue to contribute money through payroll deductions to help finance the project.

Today, visitors can tour the museum exhibits, and groups of schoolchildren routinely come to the center to learn about fire prevention. The volunteers who act as guides and instructors are extremely knowledgeable since most of them are active firefighters working at the center on their time off.

When I visited the center on a beautiful sunny day in late October, there was only one other visitor and he was on his way out. So, I was lucky enough to have Clement Thurn, a Columbus firefighter, as my personal tour guide. Clement was a pleasant middle-aged man, stocky, with a shaved head and an air of confidence that said if you ever needed rescuing from a burning building, Clement was your guy.

Clement wore dark pants and a navy polo shirt that bore the emblem of the Columbus Fire Department. As we walked among the antique horse-drawn equipment on the first floor, he told me how the Columbus Fire Department had come to be formed in 1822, following a fire that destroyed at least eight buildings. Prior to that time, firefighting companies were privately owned businesses, in competition with each other for business.

I asked Clement about the long staircase in the center of the room. There was a chain at the foot of it, and a human-size mouse mannequin wearing a nineteenth-century firefighter's uniform stood halfway up the stairs, one paw frozen in a wave— OK, that was creepy. Clement told me that the stairs led up to the second floor, where the firefighters used to live while on duty. They would be at the firehouse for six days at a time, with only one day off. That floor was not yet open to the public, but Clement hoped that it would be renovated soon and opened.

It struck me that with so many men over the years living in the firehouse around the clock, some of their spirits might still reside there, ready to spring into action at a moment's notice. At least one ghosthunter group, the Columbus-based Central Ohio Paranormal Research Group (C.O.P.R.G.), thinks so as well. They have made a few visits to the center and have recorded data indicating a haunting there. In fact, it was because of an e-mail from the group that I decided to visit the center.

I hadn't yet told Clement that I was interested in the haunted history of the place, as well as its actual history, deciding to wait a bit before springing it on him. Most of the time people speak candidly with me about paranormal subjects, but every once in awhile I run into someone who is adamantly in denial of all things paranormal; I never know when that will happen.

We were standing in the rear of the firehouse, the area that is used to instruct schoolchildren about fire prevention. The fire station's horses were kept back there, and a replica stall has been rebuilt. While we stood by the stall I told Clement why I was visiting the old firehouse.

Without hesitation, Clement said, "Oh, I believe in all that stuff," and told me that he watched all the different television ghosthunter shows. He told me that he wasn't at the fire station when C.O.P.R.G. first investigated it but that he did later hear some of the EVPs (electronic voice phenomena) that they recorded.

"What did they get?" I asked.

"Right here by this stall, they recorded strange knocking sounds," he said.

Later, I went to C.O.P.R.G.'s website and listened to the EVPs from the firehouse that they have posted there. In one of them, a C.O.P.R.G. team member asks questions of the spirits while standing by the stall. With each question she receives an immediate answer in the form of taps or knocking, perhaps on the wooden boards of the stall. The sounds are loud and distinct.

The group also recorded several good EVPs from the harness shop located directly behind the firehouse. In one of them a man's voice is picked up on a static recorder (a recorder placed in an empty room and allowed to run for awhile). The man sounds like he is in pain when he clearly says, *My headache.*

In another EVP recorded in the harness shop, a man says, *Around the steps.* Interestingly, the C.OP.R.G. team recorded feminine voices as well as masculine, a surprising finding in a place whose history was so full of testosterone. Perhaps these women's voices have nothing to do with the firehouse but are residual hauntings from another time.

I asked Clement if he had ever experienced anything unusual while he was working at the firehouse. He said that a lot of the people working there have heard footsteps and hoofbeats, and every time something goes wrong the old hands tell the newer guys that it's "only Captain D.," a reference to Captain George Noah Dukeman, who had a heart attack and died while on duty in 1939.

As we spoke, Clement showed me the children's learning center, including an eerie exhibit that shows an actual burned full-size child's bedroom with a fireman rescuing the child, the only exhibit of its kind in the country. The center's brochure provides a graphic description of the exhibit: *Get a rare glimpse into the life of a firefighter as you enter a darkened child's bedroom filling with smoke as a firefighter desperately searches for a missing child. Hear his labored breathing and muffled voice as he breathes through his self-contained breathing apparatus while crawling under the intense heat and smoke during the search.*

That exhibit is followed by one that shows that same room in the aftermath of the fire; scorched walls and ceiling, melted toys, burnt furniture, and, as the brochure reads: *most chilling of all is the silhouette of the child on the soot covered bed, an all too familiar sight to firefighters.*

Wow! I simply stood there rooted to the spot, looking through the large windows into those rooms, thinking of my own seven little grandchildren. Mentally, I thanked Clement and firefighters everywhere for the miraculous work they do; I'm only sorry I didn't speak my thanks aloud.

Clement must have understood the expression on my face because he said, "It's a great exhibit, but sometimes too intense for the really little kids, so we skip it with them. There are other exhibits that we can use to instruct them."

Focusing on why I had come to the firehouse I repeated my question about any personal ghostly experiences Clement may have had at the center.

"I did have an experience with that phone there," he said, gesturing toward a phone mounted in a closet, resembling a telephone booth. "I was alone in the museum, and I was up at the front desk when I saw the light for this phone go on."

"What did that mean?"

"It meant that someone was using the phone in the back of the building, the one in the closet but, of course, the problem was that I was the only one in the place. So, who was on the phone?"

A good question, I thought.

"I only hope the ghost wasn't making a call to China," Clement said with a smile.

Maybe Captain D. was making a really long-distance call from the great beyond.

"There was something else, too," Clement continued. "Since most of us are active firefighters we have a dispatch radio at the front desk, so we are always aware of what's going on with the department. On one of the recordings made by the ghosthunters, you hear the dispatch radio at the desk go off and right after that a male voice says, *Fuck the radio*. Must be a firefighter, I thought; only a firefighter would say that."

Maybe it was a long-ago firefighter, weary and overworked, that uttered such profanity from an unseen realm, and maybe it was a ghostly firefighter on the telephone trying unsuccessfully to call home; we'll never know for sure. But one thing is for sure—old No. 16 Engine House maintains the spirit of these old-time firefighters and, no doubt, those spirits are still very much on duty.

Legendary Ghosts:
The Blue Flame Ghost

The story says that in the 1930s a vibrant young woman lived in Sugar Grove, Fairfield County. Engaging and friendly, she fell in love with the wrong man—a hot-tempered loudmouth to whom she became engaged. Her friends noticed how her behavior and personality changed as a result of this new relationship. She never seemed to smile anymore and became cold and distant. On several occasions her friends witnessed the young woman and her fiancé having fierce arguments in public.

One night the couple parked beside the Mae Hummel covered bridge. No one knows what caused it, but a bitter altercation broke out between them. In a fit of passion, the woman drew out a knife and stabbed her fiancé in the throat. She continued hacking away at him until she had severed his head from his body.

Bleeding severely, the woman staggered down the road, carrying her fiancé's head. At some point along the road she collapsed and died, the grisly head lying beside her.

The old covered bridge is long gone—relocated to a farm in Hocking Hills—and has been replaced by a modern concrete span. But the woman's ghost still lingers there. It is said that if you stand on the bridge at night and call out the woman's name, a glowing blue form in the shape of a woman will materialize on the road and slowly drift toward you.

You might have problems summoning the ghost, however, since her real name is lost to us. So, you will have to start reciting women's names to see which one is a "hit."

Spotlight On:
Ohio Exploration Society

The Ohio Exploration Society (OES), based in Pickerington, Ohio, was originally founded by Jason Robinson in 2000 as an urban exploration group. The group began to discover haunted locations throughout the state and in 2004 started to offer paranormal investigations to the public. It has twenty-six members scattered across the state.

Conducting physical research through the use of video recorders, digital cameras, audio recorders, and other specialized equipment combined with historical research, the OES documents paranormal events without charging for its services. The group also uses the abilities of intuitive medium Larry Copeland to help in investigations.

Robinson says that the most haunted site the group has explored is the Moonville Tunnel in the now-defunct town of Moonville in Vinton County, near Athens, Ohio (incidentally, you can read about OES' work in Athens in the chapter about The Ridges). Robinson says that the Moonville Tunnel was "where I experienced the most intense moment during my eleven years of investigating the unknown."

Robinson says, "Our group was standing in the middle of the tunnel in pitch dark when a scuffling sound came down the hill just outside the east end of the tunnel. We then heard footsteps walk across the gravel and then run straight toward us. We turned on our flashlights and the running immediately stopped. We walked to the end of the tunnel where there was a 10- to 15-degree temperature drop, a consistent EMF spike, the feeling of thick static electricity, and a thick fog. All of this was followed by the smell of old musk cologne. This lasted for about one minute before dissipating. Our experience, combined with historic accounts of ghostly activity and photos and video shot by other eyewitnesses that appear to show a ghostly figure inside the tunnel, make the Moonville Tunnel a genuine haunt!"

See **ohioexploration.com** for more information about the Ohio Exploration Society.

CHAPTER 13

Ohio State Reformatory
MANSFIELD

CONSIDERING THE DESPAIR, VIOLENCE, and austere living conditions inherent in any prison, it is no wonder that the spirits of inmates often remain imprisoned behind bars long after their mortal lives have ended. There are several infamously haunted prisons in the United States—Alcatraz in San Francisco, Eastern State Penitentiary in Philadelphia, and West Virginia State Penitentiary in Moundsville, to name a few—but perhaps none as ghost-ridden as the Ohio State Reformatory in Mansfield.

In 1885 construction began in Mansfield on a new Ohio Intermediate Penitentiary, a halfway stop between the Boys Industrial School in Lancaster and the "Big Leagues" of the

Ohio State Penitentiary in Columbus. It was designed to house young first-time offenders who might yet be reformed. Perhaps to serve as inspiration for these boys, the new facility was designed in a blend of Gothic, Romanesque, and Queen Anne styles to resemble a cathedral, its towers and soaring walls constructed of large stone blocks and granite pillars. Were it not for the gates and ubiquitous iron bars, the massive building could be mistaken for an old English abbey, although some have likened the structure to Dracula's castle.

The center received its first inmates in 1896, and they were immediately put to work building the prison's sewer system and the 25-foot stone wall surrounding the 15-acre site. Construction was completed in 1910, and when it was finished the prison could boast of the largest free-standing cell block in the world, six tiers tall with 600 cells.

The incredible architecture of the prison has made it a famous location for videographers and filmmakers. It served as the prison in *The Shawshank Redemption* and also figured in *Air Force One*, *Tango and Cash*, and *Harry and Walter Go to New York*.

As in any prison, the OSR (as it's nicknamed) has seen its share of death. In 1926 an inmate shot to death a corrections officer, and in 1932 an inmate beat to death another guard in the Hole (solitary confinement) using a three-foot iron rod. A suspicious death occurred on November 6, 1950, when the wife of the prison superintendent died after being shot through the left lung. Her shooting was ruled accidental; it was said that she knocked a loaded gun off a shelf which discharged. But the fact that the superintendent was in the process of divorcing her has added another angle to her death. The superintendent himself died in his office nine years later, felled by a heart attack.

In 1955 an inmate hanged himself in his cell. Another prisoner turned himself into a human torch using turpentine and paint thinner stolen from the prison's furniture shop. Two inmates were left overnight in a cramped cell in solitary confinement. In the morning only one man walked out alive; the other's body was found stuffed beneath the bunk. In 1990 the OSR emptied its inmate population to a newly built prison and closed its doors, although the ghosts apparently forgot to relocate.

After so many years and so many people, the 250,000-square-foot prison found itself in a state of disrepair: leaking roofs, broken windows, rusting iron bars, layers of paint peeling off the walls. Now owned and operated by the nonprofit Mansfield Reformatory Preservation Society, the prison is slowly but surely coming back to life. The society offers a variety of tours and rents out the facility to ghosthunters, with the profits from these activities going to further renovate the prison.

When my Haunted Housewife friend Theresa Argie (see page 184) invited me to join her and about fifty other ghosthunters on an overnight investigation at OSR, I jumped at the chance; OSR tours fill up quickly. The OSR had long been on my list of "100 Haunted Locations to Visit Before You Die" and I had tried to get to it when I was researching *Ghosthunting Ohio* in 2003, but the staff could not seem to squeeze me into any tours. Now, seven years later, I was finally going to OSR.

It was a beautiful April evening when we all gathered beneath the stone towers of the reformatory. Besides Theresa and me, our group was fortunate to include Cathi Weber, who operates Willoughby Ghost Walk; Michelle Belanger, psychic vampire; and spirit medium Jackie Williams. After a short review of the OSR's rules, members of the society led us on a tour to familiarize us with the layout of the prison, and then we were turned loose.

Even in April, the temperature can be quite cool in the vast, unheated building, and by the time darkness fell there was a distinct chill permeating the air. It's difficult to explain the interior layout of the prison—all the various corridors, cell blocks, ancillary areas, warden's quarters, etc.—but suffice to say we had a lot of ground to cover. The good thing was that we had the entire night to explore it all.

In a facility as large as the OSR, we were able to work in small teams without interfering with each other. Knowing how competent an investigator Theresa Argie was, I worked with her team. Sometimes with large sites, investigators will set up stationary cameras and sound recorders in areas with reported paranormal activity while wandering through the building with handheld cameras and recorders. However, because of the several teams working in the building, we did not set up any stationary equipment but carried it all with us.

For better photographic opportunities, the prison "goes dark" (turns off the lights) while the teams work, which can be a scary experience in itself. Nothing gets your heart racing as much as creeping along a narrow steel catwalk six stories up with nothing but a flimsy—and rusting—iron bar between you and the dark abyss below, the only illumination coming from the weak beam of your flashlight. One slight stumble and you could become the newest ghost at OSR. This is not good news for someone who has a fear of high open spaces—someone like me.

Trying my best to swallow my fear, I inched along the catwalks of the cell block tiers, sticking as close to the iron bars of the cell as I could. In the flashlight's glow, sheets of hideous green paint peeled off the bars and walls like scabs. Debris littered many of the cells; old shoes, a shirt, rolls of toilet paper, moldy books and yellowed newspapers, scraps of note paper, all garbage left behind by the last prisoners to have inhabited the OSR, and now museum relics.

We would stop in some of the cells where one of us may have had a "feeling" that there was some energy, perhaps some

Ohio State Reformatory cell block

spirit, waiting there to make conversation. The typical method was simply to ask the spirit questions aloud while we kept our recorders on, or used a K2 meter (a device that indicates paranormal activity through lighted LEDs) or an EMF meter (a device that records electromagnetic frequency). We did not expect to hear an audible response to any of our questions. In an EVP (electronic voice phenomena) session it is more typical to hear the responses only upon playback of the recording; the K2 and EMF meters, however, do provide an instantaneous response.

Theresa and I were standing inside a cell on the lower level. I was taking pictures of her conducting an EVP session, thinking that if she was in contact with a ghost some anomaly might appear in my photos. As we stood there, Theresa asking questions, Jackie Williams came by and stopped outside the cell. Without so much as a moment's hesitation she said, "Young guy, white, blond hair. T-shirt with rolled-up sleeves," and then she continued on down the cell block.

I looked at the bunk where Jackie said the ghost was sitting and squinted in the darkness trying to see what she had seen, but to no avail. I have been on countless investigations in which at least one member of the team was blessed with this psychic vision, and I have to admit that I have been envious of those who can so easily see ghosts. I do believe that we all have some psychic abilities and that we can even train ourselves to develop them further, but I am not convinced that we can train ourselves to see ghosts. That ability may be a function of either "you have it or you don't." And I guess Jackie had it.

She came back to our cell a few minutes later and stood in the doorway, watching us. It did not seem to Theresa and me that we were getting any response to Theresa's questions from the ghost. There seemed to be no indication at all that we had actually contacted the ghost, but Jackie thought differently.

"He's angry," she said.

"What do you mean?" Theresa said.

Jackie took one step inside the cell. "He doesn't like the fact that you're asking him all these questions. He's very upset that you're asking him all that."

"What do we do?" I said.

"Well, he has a very angry expression on his face," Jackie said. "He's just not going to talk."

That sounded like a line from an old cops-and-robbers movie—*I'm no stool pigeon, I ain't going to talk, copper*—but it was at least appropriate for the place. We took Jackie's advice and quit badgering that hard-boiled ghost; there were plenty others around and maybe some that were more willing to talk.

For the rest of the night we roamed the building, spending more time in the prison chapel, the infirmary, the library, and the warden's family quarters, in addition to the cavernous dining hall and the cell blocks. Considering the grim history of the building and the several ghosts that have been discovered in some of these areas, we thought the odds of our catching one on video or voice recording were pretty good.

Unfortunately, when we concluded the investigation and later reviewed the data, we found no evidence that we had made contact with any of the OSR ghosts. Disappointing, yes, but not entirely unexpected. Sometimes, when there are large groups of people investigating a site, even one as large as the OSR, there is simply too much human interference to allow effective communication with ghosts. Often, smaller is better.

But the fact remains that many ghosthunters, as well as curious visitors to the OSR who may not consider themselves ghosthunters, have had encounters with ghosts. EVPs are commonly recorded there, and people do see apparitions. There is so much paranormal activity going on at OSR that Sherri Brake, a West Virginia ghosthunter who has made many trips to the reformatory, has written a book about the place. Brake's *The Haunted History of the Ohio State Reformatory* details all the ghostly occurrences that are everyday "life" there. If there is only one place in the Buckeye State that you visit to do some ghosthunting, it should be the Ohio State Reformatory.

CHAPTER 14

Malabar Farm

LUCAS

To him who in the love of Nature holds communion with her visible forms, she speaks a various language.

—Inscription upon Louis Bromfield's grave marker, from William Cullen Bryant's "Thanatopsis"

IN 1939 PULITZER PRIZE—WINNING NOVELIST and dedicated conservationist Louis Bromfield built a 32-room country home in Richland County's Pleasant Valley. Set among rolling hills and beautiful stands of beech, maple, and eastern hemlock, the 900-acre estate is a testament to the man who loved country life.

The house was designed by architect Louis Lamoreaux to appear as though various sections had been added onto it over a period of many years. The house is a blend of Western Reserve architectural styles and reflects Bromfield's love for the agricultural tradition of Ohio.

In his book *Pleasant Valley* Bromfield wrote: "Every inch of it [the house] has been in hard use since it was built and will, I hope, go on being used in the same fashion so long as it stands. Perhaps one day it will belong to the state together with the hills, valleys and woods of Malabar Farm." Bromfield's prophecy came true when the State of Ohio rescued the property from foreclosure in 1972 and made it an Ohio state park. Today, visitors to the park can view the operations of the working farm (in Bromfield's day visitors from all around the world came to see his agricultural and conservation experiments) and can tour the Big House, as the home is called.

With a bit of luck they may also encounter the ghosts of Malabar Farm.

Louis Bromfield died in 1956 and was buried less than a mile away from the house in the tiny picket fence–enclosed Pioneer Cemetery. That's a short walk for a ghost, and Bromfield is thought to be one of the spirits still residing at Malabar Farm. Another is that of an unidentified farmer and the third—and probably the most commonly sighted spirit—is the ghost of Ceely Rose, a notorious nineteenth-century murderess.

The Ceely Rose house is a stone's throw away from the Big House. In 1896 it was the scene of a gruesome triple murder when Ceely soaked flypaper in water in order to draw out the poisonous arsenic and then added the poison to her family's cottage cheese, murdering her mother, father, and brother. Ceely's motive was love gone bad; she had developed an infatuation with a neighbor boy named Guy Berry and told everyone that they were engaged to be married. Apparently, that was news—and not good news—to Berry. Trying to let her down kindly, Berry lied and told Ceely that her family was opposed to her marrying him. And so, the poison. Berry skipped town when he found out what had happened, no doubt fearing that he was next in line to feel Ceely's wrath and poor Ceely spent the rest of her life—forty-one years—in a mental asylum.

The Rose house is privately owned and not open to the public. Still, it is said that Ceely's ghost can be found in the barn adjacent to the Big House because some of the original timbers from Ceely's father's gristmill were used in the construction of the barn; ghosts can attach themselves to material objects for which they feel some personal connection.

The day I visited Malabar Farm was warm and sunny, not at all the kind of day on which one would expect to see a ghost. I parked my car in the Visitors' Center parking lot and toured the little museum inside. There, I bought a ticket for a tour of the Big House.

As the park ranger gave the tour group a brief introduction to the house standing on the stone front porch, I noticed a large statue of the Hindu elephant-headed god Ganesha mounted in a niche above the front door. His coat of white paint was flaking off, but his expression was still welcoming. Ganesha, the remover of obstacles. Perhaps because of his influence, the ghosts of Malabar had no difficulty in making their presence known.

We stepped inside the foyer, a beautifully designed room with twin staircases leading up to the upper floors. It was in this large foyer, standing between the staircases, that Humphrey Bogart and Lauren Bacall were married on May 21, 1945. They remained at the farm for their honeymoon, and the room in which they spent their bridal night can be seen upstairs. Bromfield had many Hollywood connections as a result of his work as a screenwriter. In fact, Malabar Farm takes its name from *The Rains Came,* a movie he worked on that takes place in the

Malabar Farm, Bromfield gravesite

fictional city Ranchipur, "located" on India's Malabar Coast.

The house is filled with furniture and personal belongings of the Bromfields, and walking through it one almost expects to bump into Louis or his wife, Mary, or any one of the several large dogs they kept, dogs that were given free rein to the house and apparently romped through it barking and baying like the Hounds of Hell.

It may not be surprising, then, that at least one person has reported seeing a dog in the house. One night in 2006, a man named Brett Mitchell was taking pictures of the house at night, aiming his camera at the window of the "red room," a room just outside Bromfield's bedroom. Although Mitchell didn't see anything in the window at the time, when he reviewed his photos, the clear and unmistakable image of a boxer dog appeared in the window.

Mitchell said, "Its clipped ears, towering on its head and fully alert to our actions. Its white chest flared out as if it was warning us not to disturb 'the boss.' And the eyes. The eyes! They tell it all. With a shimmering glare, this boxer dog will not dare allow his eternal home to be disturbed."

There are, of course, no longer any dogs at Malabar Farm, at least not any flesh-and-blood dogs.

Our tour group made it way upstairs to the author's impressive study. I love to visit famous writers' homes to see where they worked, and Bromfield's study was a treat. The large, airy room was lined with bookcases filled with the author's favorite books. A twin bed was built into one wall with an addition to accommodate the family dogs.

A huge, semicircular desk sat before luminous bay windows overlooking the rolling farmland. A large American flag stood between the desk and a red leather chair, the familiar red-white-and-blue jarring against the gray-and-white linoleum floor.

Directly behind the desk stood a small table, nestled right below the windows. Bromfield's typewriter squatted on the table along with a large bust of a man in a curly wig—Voltaire? Rousseau?—placed in position where it could look over the writer's work rolling out of the machine and give him advice.

Sensitive visitors to the Big House have felt "a presence" in some of the upstairs rooms, notably the bedrooms, the study, and the stairs. One woman reported that invisible hands pushed her on the stairs, nearly causing her to fall.

In 2004 a woman named Myrrha Lisbon reported on the ghostly event her boyfriend, an employee at Malabar Farm, had experienced one night after a day of giving house tours. He had been the only employee at the house that day and was now closing it up. He was in Bromfield's favorite room near a couch flanked by two lamps on end tables. He found a lamp on one end table turned on, even though he had not turned it on earlier in the day. He bent to turn it off and the other lamp came on.

Myrrha said, "These lamps are not switch-operated; they must be turned on manually by individual knobs. There is no way that it could happen without assistance by someone or something. By this time, my boyfriend was certain that he was not alone in the room."

The boyfriend also noticed that there was an indentation in the couch cushion, as though someone had been sitting there. Considering that the couch and lamps are located in a side of the room that is roped off to the public, it is unlikely that any human derriere left that impression.

As eerie as these incidents in the Big House might be, it seems that most of the ghostly activity at Malabar Farm occurs in the many outbuildings, especially the barn and the adjacent public restrooms.

The barn is frequently used for public performances, especially plays. A few years ago, Mark Jordan, the author of a play about Ceely Rose, had his share of run-ins with a ghost, perhaps the ghost of Ceely Rose herself. Mark noticed that one light in a string attached to the barn's rafters would slowly and steadily pulse on, off, on, off, mostly during the scene in the play in which Ceely kills her mother. An inspection of the lights revealed nothing wrong with them. Mark also had problems with the sound board.

Just a few days before the play's opening, Mark's sound system went berserk. For no apparent reason, the sound system went out entirely, even though it had been working fine previously. Mark called his technical assistant who checked each piece of equipment separately, finding them all suddenly and mysteriously inoperable. What were the odds of three pieces of equipment all dying at exactly the same time? With the rehearsal late and the looming possibility that the play might be sunk, Mark felt desperate.

Feeling a bit foolish, Mark stepped aside and said quietly, "Please, Ceely, we cannot tell your story unless you help us." When Jordan returned to the replacement equipment he found that everything was working perfectly.

"After that, I decided to take no chances," said Mark. "I made it a part of my business every night to thank Ceely for her help and cooperation, and we never had any further strange equipment problems."

Matt Roberts had an experience in the barn that convinced him that Ceely Rose was the resident ghost. He had been inside the barn when he started to become lightheaded. Matt claims to be "keen to the sixth sense" and felt a strong presence in the barn—so strong, in fact, that it drove him outside where he could get some fresh air. He described the chilling vision in his head this way: "It was a woman for sure. She was wearing a bonnet and a dress, both of the period when I guess Ceely would have been living. Both seemed to be a dark red color. All I saw past that was the look on her face, and it wasn't friendly. She had her teeth gritted and a very angry look."

After his encounter in the barn, Matt used the Internet to find out more about Ceely Rose. He had never seen a picture of her before, but when one came up on the Internet, his heart almost stopped beating. He said, "That is who I saw in the barn! So it was Ceely that I ran into! I can't believe it! That is the face that I saw, only very angry. I'm getting so chilled when I look at that picture!"

Sometimes, even when there is no wind, the barn door opens and closes. Mark Jordan recalled one night when he saw the door slowly swing open, pause for a moment, then slowly swing back, as though an unseen person had opened it, peered inside, and then closed it again. Mark said that it could be his overactive writer's imagination but he had the sense that there was a man present there, a tall, strong man wearing farm work clothes and a hat. He could not discern a face but felt that the whole image was a malevolent one.

The public restrooms adjacent to the barn, especially the women's room, may be frequented by the spirit of Ceely Rose. Several women said that they have heard banging noises inside and the sounds of other people when no one else was there. Cold spots have also been reported inside. Some of the actors and stagehands believe that the presence detected in the women's room is that of Ceely Rose and they often speak to her, asking her politely to desist from her paranormal pranks.

Malabar Farm is a tranquil and beautiful estate that had been lovingly cared for by its creator. It would not surprise me in the least if he was still on the premises, keeping an eye on things. Nor would it be a surprise to discover that he has met some of his older phantom neighbors and invited them all to the Big House.

Legendary Ghosts: Phoebe Wise

While many people know about the ghosts that haunt the Ohio State Reformatory in Mansfield, not many know of the ghost of Phoebe Wise, who can still be seen trudging along Reformatory Road outside the prison.

Born in 1850, Phoebe lived on the heights just above the prison. As a young woman she excelled academically, and by the age of fourteen was teaching music and English. Despite her intellectualism, Phoebe slowly became "eccentric," to put it kindly. When her parents died, she inherited the house and about one thousand dollars, not an inconsequential sum in those days.

Phoebe continued to live in her parents' house but was unable to maintain it. Trees and vines soon started to grow in and around the house, threatening to tear off the rear of the structure. As if that wasn't bad enough, a rumor that Phoebe had hidden a fortune in the dilapidated house began to make the rounds.

At home, Phoebe dressed in filthy men's clothes, looking more like a hermit than a young woman. For her weekly streetcar trips into downtown Mansfield, she always wore a long, ruffled yellow dress with a train, an enormous wide-brimmed hat, and worthless costume jewelry. She was quite the sight, especially as she spoke to horses and dogs, and the author Louis Bromfield remembered seeing her as a boy growing up in Mansfield and thought of her as a witch. She was a distant relative of Bromfield and he later immortalized her (pseudonymously) in some of his novels.

The rumors about her supposed treasure grew and one winter night in 1891, three armed burglars broke into the house, bound Phoebe, and tortured her by burning the soles of her feet, demanding to know the location of the treasure. Poor Phoebe gave up a diamond ring, a watch, and some cash, but that was all she had to give. The burglars tore the house apart, ripping up floorboards and smashing holes in the walls. After they left, she was able to free herself and walked down the hill to the Reformatory, where she telegraphed the police. The three bandits were eventually captured.

Now something of a celebrity, Phoebe attracted the attention of people offering her advice, business schemes, and even marriage proposals. One persistent suitor was Jacob Kastanowitz, an immigrant from Austria-Hungary who annoyed her to distraction by tapping on her windows and doors at night and following her everywhere she went. There were even a few times when he broke into her house and assaulted her. Jailed for those offenses, he would go right back at it after being released. His stalking also earned him a short stint in a mental asylum in Toledo.

Near midnight on May 22, 1898, Kastanowitz tried to break into her house through a window, supposedly yelling that she should *Marry me or kill me*. Grabbing her Winchester .32 rifle, Phoebe chose the latter option. Her single shot killed him. No charges were filed against Phoebe, and the headline in the *Mansfield Daily Shield* read: "Phoebe Wise Rids Herself of an Intolerable Nuisance."

More than ever now, Phoebe became a character. She became even more of a recluse in the tumble-down house and was rarely seen. In 1931, while she was on a rare trip to town, someone broke into her house and ransacked it, doing a great deal of damage. After that, she never left home again although she could sometimes be seen in the doorway of her home, cradling her trusty rifle, or walking down Reformatory Road to fetch water or firewood.

Phoebe Wise died in 1933. Her house was pulled down by misguided folks who still believed she had hidden a fortune in its walls. Tormented in life by burglars, stalkers, and unkind people who believed her to be a witch, or at least a crazy loon, Phoebe's spirit must not rest easy. That would be the only way to explain the ghostly image of the bent old woman that is still seen to this day creeping down Reformatory Road on dark and moonless nights.

Northeast

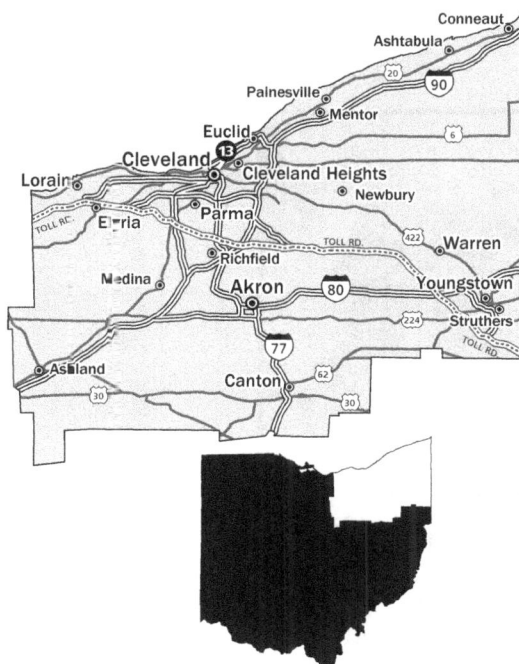

Ashtabula
   Ghosts of the Ashtabula Train Disaster

Cleveland
   Agora Theater
   Cuyahoga County Archives Building
   Franklin Castle
   Local Heroes Bar & Grill

Mentor
   Lawnfield

Newbury
   Punderson Manor

Richfield
   Stone Garden Farm & Museum

CHAPTER 15

Franklin Castle
CLEVELAND

ANY BOOK ABOUT HAUNTED OHIO LOCATIONS would be remiss if it did not include Franklin Castle, considered by many to be the most haunted building in the state. Franklin Castle's history of strange events and truly paranormal happenings, combined with rumors, fabrications, and wild tales, have also made it one of the most controversial haunted houses in the Buckeye State.

Sitting in Cleveland's Ohio City neighborhood on Franklin Avenue, the dilapidated Gothic four-story stone mansion with its boarded-up windows, steeply pitched roof, corner turret, and rusting fence looks like something right out of a Charles Addams cartoon. The architectural details of gargoyles, stone balconies, wrought-iron railings, and carved lintels all hint at the elegance and beauty for which the house was renowned when it was built in 1865 by Prussian-immigrant-turned-banker Hannes Tiedemann. But those glory days are long gone, and the crumbling house is now in danger of being torn down.

The mansion contains at least twenty-one rooms (the count varies) and features a fourth-floor ballroom accessible by its own staircase, marble fireplaces, dumbwaiters, a wine cellar, and numerous secret passageways and secret rooms hidden by concealed doors. The purpose of these passageways and rooms is unclear, but they give rise to many of the ghost stories associated with the house.

Several of the stories are related directly to Hannes Tiedemann, although many of them remain unsubstantiated. What is true is that his fifteen-year-old daughter, Emma, died in the house from diabetes and that his wife, Luise, also died in the house at the age of fifty-seven, apparently as a result of liver disease. During the Tiedemanns' tenure in the house, three of their children died, as did Tiedemann's elderly mother.

But beyond these tragic deaths, there are rumors about Tiedemann that also contribute to an explanation as to why the house is haunted. It was whispered that Tiedemann had several affairs and sexual encounters within the vast confines of the house. One persistent story says that Tiedemann hanged his niece Karen from the rafters because she was insane and he wanted to end her misery. But another version of the story says that he killed her because she was promiscuous and he found her in bed with his grandson. By hanging her Tiedemann covered up the murder as a suicide. In another story it is purported that Tiedemann accidentally killed a servant girl who was his mistress. When he discovered that she wanted to marry another man, he tied her up and gagged her; she strangled to death. In some versions of that story, Tiedemann murders the girl on her wedding day when she spurns his advances.

There is little to substantiate these stories as there is little to substantiate the discovery of a pile of baby skeletons in a small room at the rear of the house, although at one time, the house did serve as a doctor's office. Rumored to be the remains of the doctor's botched medical practices—or perhaps the result of his medical experimentation—the remains were supposedly examined by the coroner and dismissed as simply "old bones." But what did that mean? Animal bones or human bones?

One of the strangest stories about Franklin Castle has to do with its connection to a German Socialist organization. By the early 1900s Tiedemann had already sold the mansion to a family by the name of Mullhauser. They, in turn, sold the house to the German Socialist Party in 1913. The group used the house for meetings and parties, although it was largely unoccupied during the fifty years or so they owned it. There is a story that claims the German Socialists were actually Nazi spies, operating a spy ring out of the house. It is said that, during the war years, twenty members of their party were machine-gunned to death in one of the mansion's secret rooms, their bodies buried in the house. Decades later, a German short-wave radio was discovered in the rafters.

It is possible that these victims make up part of the ghostly retinue that resides in the mansion. But there is also a "lady in black" that has been seen in various rooms inside the house— some say she might be the ghost of the murdered servant girl, or possibly Mrs. Teidemann herself—as well as a "lady in white."

Among the ghosts that haunt Franklin Castle are several children; could they be the ghosts of the Tiedemann children who died in the 1880s? In the 1930s, during the time that the

Socialists owned the house, they rented part of it to an ailing attorney. A nurse who took care of the attorney recalled being terrified at night by the sounds of a small child crying. In 1968 James Romano, his wife, and six children bought the house. On the day that the family moved in Mrs. Romano sent the children upstairs to play. A few minutes later they returned, asking if they could have a cookie for their new friend, a little girl who was upstairs crying. Mrs. Romano followed her children back upstairs, but there was no little girl to be found. On several subsequent occasions the Romano children reported visits from ghostly children.

The Romano family had other encounters with the paranormal in their new house. Mrs. Romano heard organ music in the house, although the family did not own an organ, as well as footsteps tramping up and down hallways, and voices and the sound of glass clinking on the third floor when no one was there. After consulting a Catholic priest and having the house investigated by a local ghosthunting group, the Romanos had had enough. In 1974 they put the mansion up for sale.

Famed parapsychologist Hans Holzer had once visited Franklin Castle and declared that "this place was and still is haunted." But that did not deter the reverends Sam Muscatello and Tim Swope of the Universal Christian Church from buying the mansion.

Muscatello and Swope originally planned to turn the second-floor dining hall of the mansion into a church, and they hoped to set up a food bank as well, despite the presence of the ghosts. Swope spent ten weeks in the mansion alone, his radio blaring, in order to drown out the paranormal sounds echoing in the house. He often called on the spirit of Karen to make her presence known to him, especially in a third-floor room known as the "cold room" because it was at least ten degrees colder than the other rooms in the house.

Muscatello and Swope used the haunted history of the mansion as a way to raise money for their church. They began charging people to tour the haunted mansion, and it is likely that they boosted the reputation of the place by placing the "baby skeleton" bones in the house themselves.

The reverends also invited the media to investigate the house. Cleveland radio executive John Webster visited the house to conduct an on-air investigation. As he was walking up a staircase, something grabbed his tape recorder and flung it down the stairs.

"I was climbing the stairs with a large tape recorder strapped over my shoulder," Webster recalled. "I just stood there holding the microphone as I watched the tape recorder go flying down to the bottom of the stairs where it broke in pieces."

Ted Ocepec, a television reporter, saw a hanging ceiling light suddenly begin turning in a circular motion. "I just don't know," he said, "but there's something in that house."

Unable to raise the capital for their church, Muscatello and Swope sold the mansion to Cleveland Police Chief Richard Hongisto, who lived there less than a year. Michael DeVinko was the next owner of the Franklin Castle, and he sank about a million dollars into restoring the structure but was eventually forced to sell it for personal reasons.

In 1999, twenty-five-year-old Michelle Heimburger bought the mansion, paying $350,000 in cash. Heimburger was a Cleveland native but had made her fortune in Silicon Valley with an obscure little company called Yahoo! Inc. Heimburger's intention was to restore the mansion to its original glory, but only six months later an arsonist set fire to the house, causing $200,000 worth of damage. The arsonist was convicted and spent five years in jail, but the cost of repairs, in addition to the expenses she had already incurred in renovations, put Heimburger's plans on hold.

For several years the house remained vacant and slowly deteriorating. Heimburger eventually leased the house to Charles Milsaps, who intended to renovate the house and open it as a private club. But despite putting up a misleading website implying that the work had already been done and the mansion was now a snazzy, sophisticated club, very little had been done to the crumbling mansion; it did not even have running water. On his own initiative, Milsaps, who was living in the mansion's carriage house, started hosting haunted tours of the house.

I visited Franklin Castle a few years ago on a tour of haunted Cleveland. Our bus pulled up in front of the boarded-up mansion and we all got out. It was unclear whether we would be able to go inside, but a man showed up inside the gate, telling us that we were denied access to the property. Another bus pulled up and it appeared that those passengers *would* be given access. A debate between the two groups ensued, resulting in my group getting back on the bus and leaving the premises. I still do not know if the other group actually got inside the mansion.

When Heimburger heard that Milsaps was conducting haunted tours of the mansion, she had her lawyer order him to desist. Heimburger has become impatient with Milsaps' inability to deliver his promises and now wants to wash her hands of the mansion.

She may get her wish. As of September 2010, the City of Cleveland has condemned the property. Whether or not the grand old mansion will be demolished, taking its ghosts with it, or whether there may be some late-hour reprieve is anyone's guess. But stay alert; if Franklin Castle is indeed saved, it may yet be open to ghosthunters.

CHAPTER 16

Cuyahoga County Archives Building

CLEVELAND

WHAT BETTER PLACE TO STORE the historical and genealogical records of Cuyahoga County than in an elegant 1874 Victorian mansion built in the Italianate style for Robert Russell Rhodes? The beautiful red brick building, with its large windows trimmed in white stone and decorated with massive carved lintels, sits on a little hill on Franklin Boulevard NW, just a stone's throw away from the haunted Franklin Castle. A central cupola rises from the building, adding to its imposing appearance.

When Cleveland's own Psychic Sonya told me that one of the haunted places she wanted to show me was the county archives building, I immediately visualized some grim, concrete building that couldn't possibly harbor any ghosts. But when we pulled into the driveway of the stately old building and I gazed up at the large, blank windows looking down at me, I changed my mind. There just had to be ghosts inside.

We walked up the front steps and pushed open the massive wooden doors, entering into a foyer and center hall. Two beautiful rooms with high ceilings and detailed crown moldings opened on either side of us. In the room to our right, a huge gilt-trimmed mirror topped the intricately carved mantel on the opposite wall. A long table stood in the center of the room, directly below a large brass chandelier with a cluster of glass globes. I stood there, admiring the room, wondering what it would have been like to have lived in such a house.

"I had an experience with that chandelier," Sonya said, looking up.

"Really?"

"Yes, it was in 2009. I was setting up to give a lecture in the room across the hall when someone here in this room mentioned my name," Sonya said. "As soon as she said my name, that chandelier started swinging." I looked up at it again. It seemed fairly substantial to me, not anything that would move in a breeze. Maybe not even in a tornado. "And I don't mean gentle swaying," Sonya continued, "I mean back and forth." She swung her arm wildly to illustrate her point.

"It didn't stop until Judith told it to knock it off," Sonya said, referring to Dr. Judith Cetina, the County Archivist. "Another time, one of the employees who didn't believe in ghosts challenged the chandelier to move. It didn't and, thinking he had proven his point, he walked out of the room. As soon as he was gone, the chandelier started swinging."

Just as she was telling me about the incident, Leany Stevers, an archives employee, walked into the room. She and Sonya already knew each other from Sonya's many visits to the archives, both for research and to ghosthunt.

"Telling him about the chandelier?" Leany asked. "Did you tell him about the other time?"

"Not yet, but you can tell him," Sonya said.

Leany told me that she and a few other people had moved the large table that was under the chandelier to a position against the wall. They noticed that the chandelier was swaying slightly. As they watched, it picked up speed and began to swing more forcefully, finally moving quite rapidly. They moved the table back beneath the chandelier, and it gradually slowed to a stop. As a test, they carried the table back against the wall with the same results; the chandelier reacted violently to the removal of the table. Needless to say, the table is once again restored to its apparently rightful place beneath the chandelier.

Sonya and I walked through the former mansion to a back stairs that took us up to a floor where there were rows after rows of big, crumbling books cramming several rooms from top to bottom. Those half-forgotten rooms made me think of what it must be like to wander through an ancient Egyptian tomb— dusty, dim, and quiet, so quiet. I felt oddly uncomfortable roaming through those rooms, and that from a writer, a person who loves to be surrounded by books.

We passed through a set of double doors and found ourselves in a passage that led into another building, the adjoining Nelson Sanford House, built in 1862. Some of the rooms held the archives' overflow—stacks of boxes and books everywhere—but most of the rooms were empty and neglected. Beautiful marble mantels and intricate plasterwork were oddly juxtaposed with pain-flaking walls, stained floors, scratched and chipped doors. We went up another flight to more rooms, these paneled in cedar, but retreated when we came across yellow caution tape that we thought signaled weak floors. We went back down to the previous floor where sunlight only dimly flitted through the windows and shadows seemed to move in the hall. Forget what I felt in the archives building; this one was much worse.

I had been taking pictures all along, hoping to uncover something unusual, and I snapped a few last shots before we headed back through the passageway to the archives building. Back in the archives building we stopped by the stair at the rear of the building.

"This is where we saw the little boy ghost," Sonya said, referring to an incident that had occurred on one of her ghost tours of the building.

Sonya told me that on that night she had already sent one of her assistants, a big guy nicknamed Coyote, down to the basement to make sure that no undesirables broke into the building while the tour was in operation—there are better neighborhoods in Cleveland than the one in which the archives building is located, and Sonya is always concerned about matters of security on her tours.

"Tell me what happened."

"First, you should know that in the past we have heard the sound of a bouncing ball coming from this section of the building. We've heard it bounce right down these stairs," Sonya said, indicating the stairs to the basement by which we now stood. "It sounded like a child playing with a ball."

"But you never saw the child? Or the ball?" I asked.

"No, until this one night. I saw a little boy crouching right here," she said, her hand resting on the post of the railing at the head of the stairs. "He peeked out at me and then ran downstairs. I called out to Coyote to tell him that the little boy was headed his way."

As we talked, we walked down the stairs into the hall in the basement. It was half-filled with boxes and shelves full of even more boxes.

"Coyote was standing here," Sonya said, walking almost to the end of the hall. "When I called to him, he looked up the hall and saw the little boy turning the corner toward him. They were both surprised to see each other. The boy continued a few more steps, then turned and ran straight through the wall. Coyote had always been a bit skeptical but I think that night convinced him."

"Has the boy been seen since then?" I asked, looking around and taking pictures in the hall—hey, you never know what might show up.

"Well, I found this old rubber ball in one of the rooms back here and left it out for the boy to play with, along with this toy truck." It was sitting on a shelf close to the floor. "But it doesn't look like either has been moved, so I don't think he's been around lately."

We remained in the hall for a few more minutes. Sonya spoke aloud, asking if the little boy ghost was present, coaxing him not to be shy, but to come and say *hello* to us. Nothing happened, and when I reviewed my photos later, I didn't find anything unusual in them. No surprise, really, since ghosts do not necessarily perform on demand.

Sonya has seen the little boy ghost on other occasions and has tried to move him on to wherever he belongs now, but with no luck. "He told me, 'I can't leave, they're coming back for me,'" Sonya said.

"What do you think that means?"

"At one point, this house was used as an orphanage. In earlier days, parents who could not provide for their children would sometimes drop them at the orphanage. Sometimes, they claimed them later, when their situations had changed, sometimes not."

"So, you think he might be one of those children?" I asked.

"Possibly," said Sonya, "and if so, he's waiting for his parents to come back for him."

That poor little boy, I thought. His parents will never return for him and, until he realizes that sad truth, he will be stuck there for all eternity, waiting hopefully for a reunion that will never happen.

Spotlight On: Holiday Inn Express — Cleveland

Sometimes, I think that the ghosts are making it just too easy for me. I was planning on going to Cleveland for a few days to do research for this book when I heard rumors through the paranormal grapevine about the Holiday Inn Express on Euclid Avenue in downtown Cleveland being haunted. So, of course, I made reservations to stay there.

The hotel is housed in a late-nineteenth-century bank and office building. Huge Corinthian columns frame the façade, and when you enter the building you find yourself facing a small reception desk, two chairs, and a bank of elevators.

As I registered, I asked the receptionist about the hotel's haunted reputation. She answered without any hesitation, "Oh, yes, I believe the hotel is haunted. My mother used to work here too, and she said the same thing."

"What goes on here?" I asked.

"I've never seen anything myself, but there is supposed to be a ghost of a doorman that rides the elevator up and down at night. He died on the elevator. People see him on the thirteenth floor."

"You have a thirteenth floor?" I asked, surprised since so many public buildings do not—and we think we're not superstitious?

I would like to have been placed on the thirteenth floor but, unfortunately, I was given a room on the fifteenth floor. That night, however, I did go down to the thirteenth floor to see what might happen. There wasn't any lobby on that floor, only the small public area directly in front of the elevator, so I stood around for awhile waiting. Nothing happened, except that I received a few suspicious looks from other guests who wondered what I was doing hanging around on their floor. Rather than risk being ejected by the management, I returned to my room.

In the morning, I went down to the hotel's dining room for breakfast. While helping myself to scrambled eggs and bacon I spoke with a hotel employee I'll call "Rose" about the haunting. Rose had a different version of the story than did the desk clerk.

"Yes, it did happen on the thirteenth floor," Rose said, "but the story I heard said that an investor killed himself in his office on that floor. This was back in the twenties when the market crashed. He either shot himself or hanged himself, but it happened in the office."

I asked Rose what experiences people have had with the ghost and she said that they hear people walking in the hall outside their door and hear voices. Sometimes, someone or something will knock on their doors. There is never anyone in the hall when these events happen, although some people have said they have seen shadowy figures moving in the hall. She also said that people hear an elevator going up and down in that section of the hotel, but the only elevator there has been closed and inoperable for many years.

Sometimes, Rose works as the night clerk at the front desk. "I don't know how many times I've had guests from the thirteenth floor come down in the middle of the night, all frightened by what they've heard or seen," she said, "and I have to deal with them and calm them down. One time I had a lady come down who was so afraid she wouldn't go back upstairs for her belongings. We had to get them for her."

Sometime, if I'm ever back in Cleveland, I might just reserve a room on that thirteenth floor. Maybe I'll leave my door open all night and see what wanders in.

CHAPTER 17

Local Heroes Bar & Grill
CLEVELAND

IT'S FITTING THAT A BAR AND GRILL located directly across the street from Progressive Field, the Cleveland Indians' ballpark, would be named Local Heroes. It's also fitting—if you believe that Cleveland is a cursed city, as some people do—that the restaurant would be haunted. Part of that curse comes from the fact that the land upon which the ballpark stands was once a Native American burial ground, now desecrated by the ballpark. Worse, the desecration is from a team that sports a controversial and ugly Indian stereotype known as "Chief Wahoo" on its uniforms. Is there any wonder the city, and the baseball team, is cursed?

Local Heroes occupies a nineteenth-century three-story brick building on the corner of East Ninth Street and Bolivar. It's a warm and welcoming place, somehow reminiscent of TV's *Cheers* bar, minus Norm and Cliff. Brick walls with wood-paneled wainscot, high ceilings with fans, and simple wood furniture gave me the feeling of stepping back in time. Having already finished my lunch of chicken tenders and some of the best-tasting french fries I've ever eaten, I was sitting by the window, looking out at the cold, gray sky, waiting for Psychic Sonya, a well-known Cleveland psychic and tour operator of the city's more infamous haunted locations. We had first met several years before as I was researching my original *Ghosthunting Ohio* book; my wife and I had taken Sonya's tour and had thoroughly enjoyed it. Now Sonya had agreed to show me some of her favorite haunts in the Cleveland area, and Local Heroes was one of them.

When Sonya arrived a few minutes later she came well prepared. She plopped several large notebooks crammed with all her research on the table. She took off her coat, pushed back her nearly waist-length hair, and got right down to business, reviewing the places we would visit and showing me unusual photos that people had captured at them.

One of them, in particular, was highly unusual, and it gave me the creeps just looking at it. It's a photo of Sonya standing in the dusty basement of Local Heroes taken by a woman on Sonya's tour named Susan Lias. Sonya is wearing a dark dress and top and is standing facing the camera. In front of her body and to her left is a long-fingered hand. The position of the hand looks as though someone was standing behind Sonya with her arms around her.

"Holy cow," I said, immediately thinking that a writer should have a more erudite reply. "It's a hand!" *Hello, Captain Obvious.* I studied the photo and noticed that there was something at the wrist that appeared to be part of a sleeve and perhaps a wedding ring on one of the fingers.

"I was standing there in the basement when I suddenly felt that there was someone there with me, right behind me," Sonya said. "I told the people on the tour to take pictures, and this photo was the result."

I looked at the photo again. I don't know how many pur-ported ghost photos I've examined over the last several years that turned out to be fog, smoke, a smudge on the lens, a finger or camera strap partially covering the lens, condensation, you name it, but this photo was something else. I simply couldn't explain it.

"And you're sure there was no one standing behind you," I said. "I mean, no living person."

"There was no one," she said. Clearly, the photo revealed only air behind her. "We've had a lot of experiences in the base-ment."

Two women walked into the restaurant, friends of Sonya whom she had asked to join us at Local Heroes. They some-times helped her with her tours, and both had been in the base-ment several times.

One of the women, Judy Papesh, had recorded an eerie EVP on a previous visit to the basement, and Sonya asked her to play it for me. Judy dug through her skull-decorated purse, large enough to conceal a Volvo, and produced a digital recorder. She turned it on and handed it to me. I held it closely to my ear and stuck a finger in my other ear to drown out the hubbub in the bar.

I heard Judy and Sonya talking on the recorder, and maybe a few other voices, but nothing unusual. Then, just a few seconds later, a bloodcurdling, prolonged scream right in my ear jolted me in my chair. "What the hell!" I said.

The women were looking at me, smiling knowingly.

Ghost hand appearing on Psychic Sonya (Photo courtesy of Susan Lias)

"Let me hear it again."

Judy reset the recorder and handed it back to me. Even though I knew what was coming, the screaming woman still sent shock waves through me. It was apparent that no one had actually heard the scream at the time, since they continued talking as though nothing had happened. Had they really heard that scream, they would have hightailed it out of that basement pronto. I'm sure of that because I know that's what I would have done.

I gave the recorder back to Judy. "That's incredible," was all I could say.

"Ready to go down to the basement?" said Sonya.

"Yes, sure . . . why not?" I said, trying to sound like I meant it.

The bar manager unlocked the door to the basement for us. Sonya was well known there and trusted. We switched on the light for the stairs and walked down, picking our way around paint cans and other assorted junk cluttering the steps.

The smell emanating from the basement was rank, to put it mildly. Sonya explained that, for some reason, the sewer lines were not buried underground but actually ran across the basement floor and out of the building. Nice.

The basement was dry and dusty, with old brick walls and some arched vaults opening off the main corridor. Some of the vaults had been bricked in over the years, leaving only a curving line of bricks in the wall as evidence of where the opening had been. Sonya said that there were tunnels that led from the basement to the haunted Erie Street Cemetery.

The four of us walked through the basement while Sonya related some of her experiences down there. It was common for people to be touched or have their hair pulled, Sonya said. Something pulled the long ponytail of a woman on her tour, she said, and the woman's hair stood straight up for a moment before falling back down.

"We all saw it happen," Sonya said.

As a psychic Sonya has the ability to see ghosts, and she can get them to "cross over," or "go to the light"—in other words, go to wherever it is we are supposed to go after we die—but she can only do that if the ghost is willing to go. If not, it gets to remain where it is, creeping around in some dusty, stinking basement.

One such ghost is a woman, perhaps the screaming woman in the EVP, since Sonya has the sense that a woman may have been murdered in the basement, although she is still looking for documentation of that.

On one of her tours, the group of ladies heard a loud crash, like a steel door being slammed, although there were no doors to be slammed in the basement. Sonya asked the ghost to do it again and, sure enough, the crashing sound came again, at which point, the women screamed and ran away. Sonya chased after them, trying to explain that the ghost only wanted to make contact with them. She caught up with them near the stairs.

Sonya said that she could see the ghost—a woman—drawing near to where the group stood, although none of the other women could see her. Sonya asked the ghost to say something and a high-pitched squeaky *Hi* floated out of the darkness. Then the ghost banged on a metal locker standing against the wall and that was about all the group could take; they were out of the basement in an instant.

Sonya does not know the identity of the female ghost and the spirit refuses Sonya's help to move on. For whatever reason, she chooses to remain there, perhaps trying to tie up the loose ends of some bit of unfinished business in her previous life. Perhaps if you are lucky enough to get to Local Heroes you may be able to lend the poor ghost a helping hand.

Legendary Ghosts: Joc-O-Sot

This "legendary" ghost was a real person who now lies beneath the grass in Cleveland's Erie Street Cemetery, founded in 1826. A Native American originally from what is today Minnesota, Joc-O-Sot fought against American forces in the Black Hawk War of 1830, the same war in which Abraham Lincoln served in an Illinois militia regiment for four months without ever being in combat. Joc-O-Sot was shot during the war but survived his wounds.

After the war, in an effort to raise money to support his tribe, Joc-O-Sot joined a vaudeville troupe in Cleveland. The troupe toured in England and there he became ill, apparently as a result of the wound he had sustained in the war ten years earlier. Realizing that he was dying, Joc-O-Sot returned to the United States and expressed his desire to be buried in his tribal homeland with his ancestors. That wish did not come true; Joc-O-Sot died in 1844 in Cleveland's Warehouse District and was interred in the Erie Street Cemetery.

Joc-O-Sot's original tombstone was a full-length stone slab placed on the ground. That stone remains there still but it is shattered in several large pieces, apparently Joc-O-Sot's revenge for having his last wish denied.

Joc-O-Sot's ghost is still seen wandering the cemetery grounds and sometimes he visits the nearby Cleveland Indians baseball stadium.

Another Native American is buried beside Joc-O-Sot. Thunderwater was born on the Tuscarora Reservation in New York in 1865 to an Osaukee mother and Seneca father. He traveled with Buffalo Bill Cody's Wild West Show and settled in Cleveland in the early 1900s. Thunderwater became a successful businessman and a champion of Native American rights and welfare; each year he conducted a memorial service at the grave of Joc-O-Sot. Thunderwater died in 1950.

It is widely believed that Thunderwater served as the inspiration for the Cleveland Indians' mascot Chief Wahoo. If he was, indeed, the inspiration for that racist emblem, then there is no doubt that both he and Joc-O-Sot haunt the ballpark and perhaps, just perhaps, they may be the cause of the Cleveland Indians' dismal record. Revenge is sweet.

CHAPTER 18

Agora Theater
CLEVELAND

IN 1966, HENRY LOCONTI SR. opened the original
Agora Theater near Case Western Reserve University. Over the
years, another dozen Agora clubs opened across the country,
but the Cleveland venue remained the grande dame. Such well-
known groups as the Buckinghams, The Pack (later Grand Funk
Railroad), The Outlaws, ZZ Top, Rainbow Canyon, James Gang,
Glass Harp, Foghat, and The Raspberries achieved national and
international prominence after getting their big break playing
the Cleveland Agora stage.

The Cleveland Agora relocated a few times, the final move
to its present location on Euclid Avenue precipitated by a fire in

1984. Its present location was once the Metropolitan Theater, opened in 1910, and walking through the Agora's doors is like taking a step back in time. Live concerts are still performed on the massive stage, framed on either side by balcony box seats. In every respect, the theater is perfectly equipped for any kind of production—from drama to rap—but there is one item missing.

There is no ghost light.

I was visiting the empty theater with Psychic Sonya and Hank LoConti. Sonya and I followed Hank through the dark theater as he switched on a few lights for us. It was afternoon and the theater was closed but Hank was gracious enough to unlock it for us. We were standing in the dimly lit backstage area, surrounded by pulleys and ropes, while high above us, catwalks seemed to float in the darkness.

"Hank, do you realize you do not have a ghost light?" Sonya said. I looked around and sure enough, no light.

"What's a ghost light?" Hank asked, nonchalantly.

"It's a light that's always kept burning on the stage," Sonya said.

"Why?" Hank asked, flipping on a light.

"It keeps the ghosts away so they won't ruin a production," Sonya said.

"The tradition goes back to Shakespeare's time," I said, "maybe before."

"No, never heard of it," Hank said.

I was surprised that he had been in the entertainment business for so long and yet didn't know about the ghost light. Is it possible that if a ghost light had been on stage there would not have been a fire in the previous location? Even more, would a ghost light have kept the ghosts that presently haunt the theater at bay?

"Well, there are ghosts here," Hank said. "I've never seen them, but I feel them around."

Hank may not have seen the ghosts, but Sonya has and some people on her tour, which makes a stop at the Agora, have also seen them. Sonya told me that one day when she arrived at the theater she saw a woman in a blue dress standing outside the door. The moment the woman saw Sonya she approached her and said, "Get rid of her."

Sonya recognized that she was talking with a ghost. "Who are you talking about?" Sonya said, calmly, as if she talks to ghosts every day . . . oh, wait, she does.

"The cleaning lady," the ghost replied, "the cleaning woman that fell. Get rid of her."

Sonya had no idea what the ghost was talking about and she vanished before Sonya could ask any more questions. Sonya went inside the theater and asked the manager if she knew anything about a "cleaning woman that fell." According to the manager there was a story about a cleaning woman back in the 1920s who was cleaning one of the box seats in the balcony; somehow, she fell out of the box and was killed.

The manager went on to say that some people have seen the ghost of the cleaning lady a few times. One of the most notable appearances was when a photographer was working in the theater, taking photos of the stage. As he was setting up, a woman wearing a light blue dress and white apron was cleaning the stage. The photographer politely asked her to step off the stage as he was about to take some pictures. The woman ignored him. He repeated his request with the same ignored result. Frustrated, the photographer went out to the manager's office to complain about the woman who was ruining his shots. The manager replied that there was no cleaning staff working that day. The confused photographer returned to the stage and saw the woman still there. In an angry voice, he ordered her off the stage. The cleaning lady looked up and then vanished. There is no record of what the photographer did next, but one can easily imagine a hasty retreat.

Agora Theater balcony

"How did you know about the cleaning lady?" the manager asked Sonya.

"Another ghost told me," she said.

There is another ghost in the Agora that Sonya calls the "man in the yellow slicker."

A while back a security guard was making the rounds one night when he heard a loud crash come from the basement. He went down to check it out, walking around in the dark with his flashlight, but he didn't see anyone. He paused in the basement and suddenly sensed someone standing behind him. He turned quickly and there, in the flashlight's glow, saw the ghost wearing a yellow rain slicker. Before the security guard could move a muscle, the ghost disappeared.

Sonya thinks the ghost in the yellow slicker might be the

spirit of a railroad worker killed on the tracks that run nearby the theater. At times it seems as though the ghost is carrying a lantern, the kind one would associate with the railroad.

Some people on Sonya's tour have taken photographs in the basement that revealed strange anomalies that might be the yellow slicker ghost.

There is also a tunnel that runs beneath the Agora, and it is designed in such an unfortunate way that in order to turn on the lights in the tunnel one has to walk the length of the tunnel in the darkness to get to the light switch. A theater manager once went down to the tunnel and started to walk through the dark to the other end. Her heart was jackhammering in her chest as the tunnel always made her nervous and she didn't like being in the dark. She hadn't gone too far into the tunnel when the lights suddenly came on. Far from comforting her, the flash of light terrorized her since she had not turned the lights on and she was clearly alone in the tunnel, except for the ghost, of course.

It is thought that ghosts draw on all kinds of energy in order to "live," even the energy associated with human thoughts and emotions. Could it be that the ghost in the tunnel tuned in to the manager's fear and used that energy to help it manipulate the lights?

The ghost in the yellow slicker does not confine himself to the basement. In fact, oftentimes he is backstage, the catwalk high above the stage apparently one of his favorite spots. No doubt, he would get a great view of any of the bands playing the Agora from that location. Sonya has tried on several occasions to help the ghost cross over to whatever realm awaits us after death, but he has been resistant.

"I've tried," she said, "but he just won't leave."

A ghost may not want to leave this earthly plane because it has some "unfinished business," something important it wanted to do in life but was unable to accomplish before death. Or it may still feel attached to family members or other people, believing they just can't get along without it. Possibly, the ghost may simply be afraid to cross over, especially if it led a less than exemplary life and now fears possible divine retribution. Sonya does not know why the yellow slicker ghost refuses to move on, but he's been stubborn.

Sonya thinks there may also be a more elusive ghost in the Agora, that of a young woman who may have been a murder victim. In the 1930s the body of a woman, most likely a prostitute, was found by the railroad tracks near the theater. The murderer had strangled her with her red fishnet stockings. Sonya senses the ghost is in the basement; perhaps future tours will discover more about her.

The Agora Theater remains a favorite stop on Psychic Sonya's tours, and as long as there is no ghost light placed on the stage to ward them off, the ghosts of the Agora will be performing right through to the final act.

Spotlight On: Psychic Sonya's Haunted Cleveland Tours

Sonya Horstman, known throughout the Cleveland area as Psychic Sonya, is an ordained Spiritualist minister with the Church of Radiant Lights in Rittman, Ohio. A natural-born intuitive psychic, Sonya became aware of her psychic abilities at an early age. One of her unique talents is clairvoyance, which explains her ability to see visions of the future. Sonya can also read a person's energy field, or aura, through her inherited Native American medicine gift of hand-trembling. Her paranormal abilities allow her to see and communicate with ghosts and to banish unwanted spirits from haunted locations.

Since 2002, Sonya has operated Haunted Cleveland Tours, which offers a variety of walking or motor coach ghost tours in Cleveland, as well as in Medina, Cuyahoga Valley National Park, and Lorain County. Some of the more notable stops on her Cleveland tour include Local Heroes Bar & Grill, Erie Street Cemetery, the Agora Theater, and Franklin Castle (see chapters in this book for all three locations)

For more information about Psychic Sonya and her ghost tours, see **hauntedclevelandtours.com,** or contact her at:

Sonya Horstman
MPO Box 154
Oberlin, OH 44074
psychicsonya@oberlin.net, (440) 775-1217

CHAPTER 19

Lawnfield

MENTOR

OHIO HAS CONTRIBUTED EIGHT NATIVE SONS
to the White House, more than any other state. One of these was
James A. Garfield, who was elected to the presidency in 1880.

Garfield was born in Cuyahoga County in 1831, the last president to be born in a log cabin. His father died when Garfield
was only eighteen months old, but despite that loss, he managed
to earn enough money for an education by driving canal boat
teams. Graduating from Williams College in Massachusetts, he
returned to Ohio to teach Classics at the Western Reserve Eclec-
tic Institute (later renamed Hiram College) and in the following
year was named its president.

The professor was elected to the Ohio Senate as a Republican in 1859, but when the Civil War broke out, he volunteered and led a brigade against Confederate troops at Middle Creek, Kentucky. He was promoted to Brigadier General at the age of thirty-one and then to Major General.

In 1862, Garfield was elected to the U.S. House of Representatives. Abraham Lincoln persuaded him to resign his commission in the army, saying that he could always find able generals to conduct the war but that he needed stalwart Republicans to support him in Congress. Garfield went on to serve in Congress for eighteen years until he was nominated to run for president at a deadlocked Republican convention in 1880. In a narrow victory against Democrat Gen. Winfield Scott Hancock, Garfield became the twentieth President of the United States.

In his brief term in office, Garfield worked to eliminate graft and corruption in the public administration and helped to restore some of the dignity and respect of the presidency that had been lost during the Reconstruction era.

On July 2, 1881, while waiting for a train in a Washington train station, Garfield was shot by a demented assassin, a frustrated office-seeker. Mortally wounded, Garfield lay in the White House for weeks, his wife Lucretia by his side. Alexander Graham Bell designed an induction-balance electrical device with which he tried to find the bullet lodged in the president's body, but without success. On September 6, Garfield was moved to the New Jersey shore, in hopes that the seaside air might help his recovery. He seemed to be recuperating for a few days, but then infection set in and he began to hemorrhage internally. On September 19, Garfield died.

Much of James and "Crete" Garfield's life was spent pleasantly at their home in Mentor. The rambling, two-and-one-half-story house was much smaller when it was originally built in 1832 by James Dickey. When the Garfields purchased the house

President James Garfield

in 1876, they added eleven rooms to the existing nine to accommodate their growing family.

The railroad ran right behind the Garfield property, and during the 1880 election thousands of admirers would stop at the house and walk down a short lane to hear Garfield give speeches from the porch of the house, the original "front porch campaign." The house earned the name Lawnfield from the many newspaper reporters who literally camped out on the lawn during the campaign.

Today, the house is a National Historic Landmark open to the public. There were only three other people on the tour the day I stopped in to see the house. And what a grand house it is!

Filled with Victorian-era furniture, the large, spacious rooms are surprisingly bright, with sunlight streaming through the many windows. The millwork in the house is beautiful; everywhere one looks, there are crown moldings, window and door trim, built-in cabinetry, all done up in warm, honey-colored wood. The multileveled center staircase, featuring a fireplace at its base, is finely crafted of that same exquisite wood.

Bibliophile that I am, however, the room that captivated me the most was the elegant library upstairs. A large, inviting fireplace, comfy chairs, wood-paneled ceilings, rows of windows, bookcases crammed with the many volumes of Garfield's library—a book lover's nirvana.

The house was so warm and inviting, so homey, that it was hard for me to believe that it was haunted. But it was. Typical of National Park Service rangers, the ranger conducting my tour was mum when asked about ghosts. I had encountered this official reticence before at the Abraham Lincoln homestead in Springfield, Illinois, when my question about ghosts almost resulted in me being escorted out of the house. But these rangers see and hear things the public does not and once they are no longer associated with the National Park Service, their tongues seem to loosen. For many years, Mark Nesbitt was a park ranger at the Gettysburg battlefield; today, he is the author of several books about Gettysburg ghosts and the owner of Ghosts of Gettysburg Tours.

But the Lawnfield ranger wasn't talking. It is believed that the ghost associated with the house is not that of James Garfield but of his wife, "Crete." Lucretia was not only a wife to him, but she also was a soul mate. The two met in school in Hiram and married in 1858. They shared the same intellectual pursuits—James Garfield spoke eight languages—attending literary circles together, traveling together, and living inseparably from each other, except when circumstances such as Garfield's military duty dictated otherwise. After her husband's murder, Lucretia added another library and vault to the house and meticulously collected and preserved all of Garfield's books, letters, and papers, establishing, in effect, the first presidential library. She continued this work for thirty-six years, until she died in 1918.

It would make sense that a woman so devoted to her husband's memory and to her home would not want to leave them.

There was a small room upstairs in the house that Lucretia used to compose correspondence. It wasn't much larger than a closet and held a writing desk and chair and little else. She would sometimes spend hours there, answering letters from her husband's friends and fans. Standing in that little room, gazing at the desk, I could almost see Lucretia busy at her work. Indeed, some people have said that they have seen her doing just that.

During renovations to the house, workers would leave their tools and equipment scattered around in the work area. When they would return the next day they would find their equipment neatly in place. That sounds like the kind of attention to a tidy and orderly house that Lucretia Garfield would demand.

The Garfields' first child, a daughter, died in 1863, and a two-year-old son died in 1876, the year in which they purchased the house. Could it be that the spirits of these children are still in the house? Visitors frequently feel as though they are being watched; could that be inquisitive children? Lucretia?

Although most paranormal investigators believe it is Lucretia that haunts Lawnfield, might there not be a case made for the presence of James Garfield as well? By the end of the Civil War in 1865 there had been more than 620,000 lives lost. Many of the widows, parents, and family members who had lost loved ones in the conflict turned to Spiritualism as a way of getting in touch with their dearly departed. Garfield first came into contact with Spiritualism while living in Hiram, Ohio, and believed that he had contacted his father, Abram, a

Depiction of Garfield assassination

man he hardly knew since Abram died when Garfield was only eighteen months old.

Further, Garfield's Secretary of State Robert Todd Lincoln told Garfield about his *own* father's death premonition. Perhaps influenced by that story, Garfield, too, had a premonition about his own death.

Would it not make sense that a man so attuned to the spiritual side of human existence would try to reach out from beyond the grave to communicate with those still earthbound?

Security guards at Lawnfield have reported hearing footsteps in the house at night when it is closed and have seen lights turn on after the guards have turned them off. Whether these strange happenings can be attributed to Lucretia, the Garfield children, or the former president himself, witnesses all feel that they are not to be feared, that they represent the loving actions of a close-knit family that is still comfortable in their beloved home after all these years. No doubt, these ghosts would welcome you with open arms.

Spotlight On:
Willoughby Ghost Walk

While it seems that every town in Ohio has its own home-grown ghost tour, there are some that offer more for the would-be ghosthunter than others. Cathi Weber's Willoughby Ghost Walk in northeast Ohio is one of those.

The Ghost Walk is a guided walking tour through the haunted historic district of downtown Willoughby, beginning at Cathi's store on Erie Street, The Spice Peddler. The tour covers approximately twelve blocks and takes about ninety minutes.

"Willoughby used to be a rough town," Cathi told me. "Many of the basements of the stores are connected and used to be speakeasies, brothels, and numbers rackets back in the twenties and forties."

Some of the haunted places on the Ghost Walk include the Willoughby Brewing Co., where female servers often report being touched by randy ghosts, and Willoughby Coal, where the body of Don Norris was found in 1947 after he supposedly fell through a small, round window high up in the building. One glance at the window and where it is located in the building and one can only say, "No way."

A favorite stop on the tour is Willoughby Cemetery, where a marker dedicated to the "Girl in Blue" memorializes the strange death of a young girl whose identity remained unknown for many years. It reads: "In memory of the Girl in Blue – killed by a train December 24, 1933 – Unknown But Not Forgotten."

Here is an account of the unfortunate girl's story, published in 1946 in The Cleveland News, written by reporter Harry Christiansen: "From where the Girl in Blue came is a mystery. At 3 a.m. she stopped at Mrs. Mary Judd's tourist home on Second St. and rented a room. She was pretty, and about 20 years old. Next morning she arose, and asked if there were any church services in town. She was dressed in blue — coat, hat, sweater, scarf. Her eyes were also blue. She said 'Merry Christmas' to Mrs. Judd and walked into Second St. A few minutes later she was seen walking into the path of the train. All attempts to prove her identity failed. Almost 50 people came to the funeral parlors, but they didn't know her. The citizens of Willoughby donated a small plot of ground in the village cemetery, and her secret went to the grave with her."

Some say that the "Girl in Blue" does not rest easy in her grave and that she still walks among the living, searching for something or someone.

Willoughby is a quaint little town, a nice place to visit. The fact that it contains such interesting spirits just makes it that much more interesting. For more information, see **willoughbyghostwalk .com.**

CHAPTER 20

Punderson Manor

NEWBURY

IN 1802 LEMUEL PUNDERSON AND HIS WIFE, SYBAL came west from Connecticut and settled on land that is now Punderson State Park, where they built a gristmill and distillery. When the couple died, they were buried at the southern tip of what is now known as Punderson Lake. Their heirs sold the property to W. B. Cleveland, who sold it to Karl Long in 1929. Long, a wealthy industrialist from Detroit, built a twenty-nine-room, fourteen-bath Tudor-style mansion that today comprises the bulk of the state park's Punderson Manor. It is unclear if Long was also responsible for the ghosts that roam not only the halls of the manor but also the grounds of the park itself.

Peter J. Donnelly had only recently arrived at Punderson as the new general manager when I made my visit to the park in August 2009, so he had not had time to experience any paranormal events for himself, although he had stories to tell.

We sat at a table in the dining room. It was a mid-afternoon weekday so the dining room was empty, which afforded us an unobstructed and beautiful view of the lake. Peter was a thin, energetic man, with close-cropped hair. Dressed in a white shirt and tie, he spoke enthusiastically about the mansion and its ghosts. He explained that the dining room was part of the original building and pointed out the section where the Cleveland family—who regained possession of the mansion after the Depression ruined Long and he died—took their meals. A stone wall set with latticework windows separated this section from the rest of the room; in Cleveland's time, that wall was an exterior wall.

"Imagine having your breakfast served to you out here with that view," he said, gesturing to the lake behind us.

"Nice to be rich." I said, thinking of my own breakfast view of my driveway and my neighbor's whining German shepherd. "Let's talk about the ghosts. What do you know about them?"

"Apparently, lots of people see things and experience strange things here. They'll mention electrical appliances that turn on even when unplugged, or they'll say they hear children running around in the halls when there is no one there. Sometimes, guests will leave their rooms and when they return, find their windows left wide open, and that in the dead of winter."

"Do you believe the manor is haunted?" I asked.

That question led us into a long and interesting conversation about ghosts, spirits, and the afterlife. Peter said that he was open to the possibility that spirits exist and told me a personal story about his mother, who was dying of cancer. He said that the night before she died, she and Peter's father were watching television when she suddenly got up and left the room. When she did not return after a few minutes her husband went to look for her and found her outside in the driveway. He asked her what she was doing out there and she replied that she had come out to speak with the "beautiful children" she had seen through the window; no one else saw the children.

It was obvious as he spoke that Peter was both moved and mystified by his mother's experience. "Maybe those children were angels," Peter said. "I don't know. I'm first generation Irish-American, and in the Old Country people would readily recognize that event.

"There is someone you should speak with, however. Nick Fischbach has been a park ranger here for many years and I know he's had some interesting experiences. I can set up a meeting with him, if you like."

"That would be great."

We shook hands and, just before he left, Peter gave me a CD of photos that a guest had taken at Punderson. "I didn't see anything on it, but it's yours. See what you find."

I was booked for two nights at the manor and was lucky enough to have a room in the old section of the hotel, part of the original family manor. I immediately went up the circular staircase to my room, a large comfortable room with a couch that I plopped onto to view the CD in my laptop. I was disappointed to see only a series of night photos featuring blurry lights from the hotel. They were all exterior shots and terribly executed; a blind man could have taken better photos. I hoped these were not indicative of what was to come.

I took a walk around the grounds to get the feel of the place. Behind the hotel was a terrace and beyond that a broad lawn that sloped down to the lake. There were some benches placed out on the lawn and I could see a path at the edge of the lawn that led into the woods along the lake. A flock of geese strutted across the grass. I walked around to the front of the building,

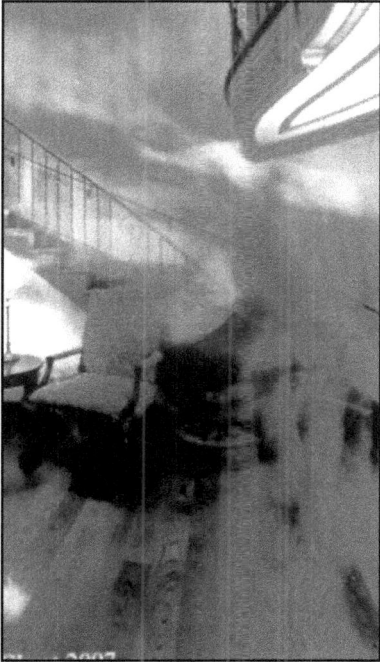

Punderson Manor ghost

admiring the timber and stucco exterior and the red, purple, and white flowers planted along the walk. This was my kind of haunted house, I thought.

That evening I had dinner in the hotel dining room. I can't remember what I ate, but I do remember that it was delicious and that the hotel featured homemade desserts, my gastronomical Achilles' heel. I also had the opportunity to chat with my server, a young woman named Maggie.

Like Peter, Maggie had not experienced anything out of the ordinary at the hotel, although she did tell me that another server once heard a woman call her name, even though no one else was in the room at the time.

After dinner I went back up to my room and awaited the arrival of a paranormal investigator friend, Theresa Argie. Theresa was a member of the Paranormal Researchers of Ohio (PRO) and a thorough and skilled investigator. Since she lived nearby, she agreed to help me investigate the hotel. When Theresa arrived, we spent some time wandering around inside the hotel taking photos and getting familiar with areas in which we might want to focus. It was dark by the time we went outside and made our way down the path through the woods to the lake. Over the years, several people had drowned in Punderson Lake, a glacial lake with a depth of 72 feet, so it's no wonder that some of the ghosts were seen there. The path led to a fishing pier in the lake. From the pier we had a great view of the manor on the hill, its lighted windows shining like yellow eyes in the dark. There may have been spirits there, but all we encountered that night were swarms of man-eating mosquitoes, so we made a hasty retreat back to the hotel.

I was to meet with Nick Fischbach the following day, so Theresa agreed to return the next night with all her equipment so that we could conduct a more thorough investigation based upon what I learned from Nick.

I learned a lot from Nick.

We met for lunch in the dining room the next day. Nick was a friendly, stocky guy with gray hair, moustache, and glasses who reminded me something of Wilford Brimley; I thought he even sounded like Brimley, too. Now Regional Manager, Law Enforcement Supervisor, Nick had been an officer in the Division of Parks and Recreation for over thirty years, twenty-five of those years at Punderson.

Nick was the kind of no-nonsense guy who told me his stories in a straightforward manner. He knew what he had seen and what he had experienced. He told me about a 1979 experience, during which the hotel was closed.

"It was raining cats and dogs," Nick said, "and me and another ranger, Dave Landen, went inside the hotel to check it out, as we did periodically. We entered the building, locked the door behind us, and noted that the inside temperature was seventy degrees. We walked up the circular staircase in the lobby and felt a sudden temperature drop. By the time we reached the top of the stairs, it was cold enough to hang meat. We could see our breath in the air.

"Suddenly, a cold wind passed right through us and we heard a woman's high-pitched laughter, really loud, and then, just as suddenly, the wind was gone and we were warm again."

"Was there a woman?" I asked.

Nick shook his head. "No, the hotel was actually shut down at that time. It was completely empty. I had always laughed off the experiences of other people, but I believe that was a spirit."

Nick also told me about a 2004 meeting he was to have with the hotel manager. "It was in November, about 3 p.m. and it was cold and spitting rain. I was at the front door about to enter the hotel when I saw an old man with fluffy hair walking quickly toward me. Despite the weather, he was wearing a white shirt with the sleeves rolled up and dress pants. I can still see him plain as day. I said, 'How you doing?' to the man, then looked down to check my watch. When I looked up a second later the man was gone."

Nick was obviously confused by this event, but even more so when he entered the hotel and one of the hotel employees asked him what he was doing outside.

"What do you mean?" Nick said.

"We saw you standing out there, looking around for something and talking to someone, but there wasn't anyone else there with you. What was all that about?"

Nick still doesn't know what it was all about.

I asked Nick what he knew about any ghosts in the lake, especially one that has been named the Blue Lady. He told me that in the 1970s a young woman drowned in the lake in a boating accident. A band of Romanian gypsies used to camp at the lake every summer, but after the girl's death, the gypsy leader, a man with the odd name of Peaches Frank, told Nick that the band was leaving and that they would never return.

Peaches told Nick that three old gypsy women were walking by the lake when they saw a young woman rise up out of the lake and come toward them. She was crying. The women recognized her as a ghost and told her to go back to the lake, which she did. That was enough for them, Peaches said, they were out of there.

The gypsies have never returned to Punderson.

There were more stories about a mysterious black cat that appeared out of nowhere, about an officer from the sheriff's department whose dog was too terrified to go down the stairs into the hotel's basement kitchen when a prowler alert sounded, about a waitress who was taking a nap on a couch when she was awakened by the sounds of invisible children running in the hall, about a couple who saw a cute, smiling little girl on the circular staircase who disappeared moments later.

Despite all that, Nick says, "I feel comfortable here. I don't worry about any of that stuff. This place grows on you, it really does."

That night, Theresa Argie returned. The weather was terrible; thunder, lightning, and heavy rain, actually great weather for hunting ghosts. This time we made a more thorough investigation, setting up cameras in the upstairs hall, the library, and the circular staircase. In addition, we used digital recorders, hoping to record some EVPs (electronic voice phenomena) in the building.

Theresa is an expert investigator, and I trusted her instincts and know-how. Still, it seemed as though we did not have any positive results from our investigation. Sometimes, though, the data needs to be reviewed several times, so who knows? We may yet find evidence of the Punderson ghosts on the tapes or recordings.

And if we don't, take a look at the photo of the circular staircase Nick gave me. It was taken by a prominent guest who has asked to remain anonymous. I'm not certain that I've ever seen a better photo of a ghost.

Spotlight On: PRO

Paranormal Researchers of Ohio (PRO) is one of the most well respected and longstanding paranormal teams in the field, covering the Northeast Ohio area and beyond. The four-member core team is supported by additional investigators and researchers when needed.

The members of PRO are dedicated to helping the public understand the paranormal world through research, investigation, and education. The group holds seminars and workshops year-round throughout the Greater Cleveland area.

Although private home investigations make up the majority of its case work, PRO often investigates public buildings and historic locations. PRO holds the distinction of being a TAPS family member and, as an affiliate member, often takes cases referred to it by The Atlantic Paranormal Society.

. Theresa Argie, a founding member of PRO, says that one of the group's favorite haunted locations is the Ohio State Reformatory in Mansfield (see the chapter in this book about the OSR). She says that it was there that PRO conducted one of its "most paranormally active and historically profound investigations."

For more information about PRO, visit **paranormal researchersofohio.com.**

Legendary Ghosts: Esther Hale

In August 1837, in the now abandoned town of Sprucevale in Columbiana County, young Esther Hale happily prepared for her wedding day. In her cabin near Beaver Creek, Esther, attired in her wedding gown, spent most of the morning arranging the wedding decorations and dreaming of her bright future with her husband-to-be.

Her fiancé's name is lost to history, as are the reasons for his absence on that auspicious day, but as the day dragged on and it became apparent to poor Esther that her young man had jilted her, she pulled shut the drapes in her cabin, locked the door, and withdrew from the world.

After several days' absence Esther's friends decided to look in on her. When they arrived at the cabin they found a sullen Esther sitting among the wedding decorations, still dressed in her wedding dress. They encouraged her to come out with them but she refused and asked them to leave. Reluctantly, they departed without her.

From time to time friends would drop by to check on Esther. They would always find her alone, sitting among the deteriorating wedding decorations. And always, she was wearing her wedding gown. Although her friends could get her to eat a little they were never able to get her to remove the gown.

Several months later, a passerby noticed the door to Esther's cabin standing ajar. Alarmed by the snowdrifts he saw that had built up inside the doorway, the man notified authorities. When law officers arrived at the cabin, they found Esther's decaying body lying on the floor, still dressed in her wedding gown.

Shortly after Esther's funeral—a funeral in which she still wore her gown—people began to see her ghost. Today, it is reported that motorists crossing the bridge over Beaver Creek, near where Esther's cabin had once stood, sometimes have a run-in with the ghost of Esther Hale. The decaying figure of a woman in a tattered white dress lunges at their cars. It should come as no surprise that this grotesque spirit makes her appearance only on August 12th, the date of Esther's ill-fated wedding.

CHAPTER 21

Stone Garden Farm & Museum
RICHFIELD

YOU HAVE TO ADMIRE JIM FRY. He's the kind of guy who believes there is still mystery in the universe; anything is possible. So when Jim tells you that strangers sometimes appear at his organic farm to offer their help, strangers that might be from the afterlife, or from a parallel universe, or perhaps, from another planet, you believe him, just like that.

I first met Jim through Psychic Sonya. She had been kind enough to show me some of the most haunted locations in Cleveland, and she suggested a drive out to her friend Jim's Stone Garden Farm.

There was at least half a foot of snow on the ground and snowflakes swirled in the leaden sky as I followed Sonya's truck over winding roads through the Cuyahoga Valley National Park (yes, there is a National Park in Ohio). We made a brief stop at the Everett Road covered bridge, originally built in 1877. In the late nineteenth century John Gilson, a local farmer, was try- ing to cross the bridge in his buggy, his wife beside him. Flood waters made the crossing difficult and, for some unknown rea- son, the horses bolted, throwing Mrs. Gilson out of the buggy. She was the lucky one; the crazed team dragged the buggy and poor John into the raging waters, where they all drowned. Searchers recovered John Gilson's body four days later. Since that time the bridge has been reconstructed, but that makes no difference to John's ghost. He haunts the bridge to this day, with people witnessing orbs and strange shadows.

Just across Everett Road is a steep path with steps that lead up and over a ridge. The path was originally made by area Indi- ans thousands of years ago. The Indians have not left. People sometimes see the spectral figures of Indian runners darting along the path through the woods.

Following Sonya, I turned into a snowy lane off Southern Road, my little Honda Civic struggling for traction as we drove up to the farmhouse. We parked in the yard and got out of our vehicles, sinking into shin-high snow. A man bundled up in winter clothing was chopping firewood, pieces of freshly split wood littering the snow around him.

"Might want to step back," Jim said by way of greeting, bring- ing the ax down again and neatly cleaving a piece of wood. I caught a glimpse of glasses and a salt-and-pepper beard beneath the hat and hood as I backed away.

"Be right with you," Jim said. "Feel free to look around in the meantime."

Sonya had been to the farm several times before, and she showed me around. Although Jim grew organic vegetables on the farm, it was clear that his passion was directed more toward re-creating a nineteenth-century village on the grounds. Over several years Jim had purchased old, historic buildings—most of them in bad condition—and had meticulously taken them apart board by board and then transported them to his farm, where he rebuilt and restored them. Now, as Sonya and I trudged through the snow, we passed by a general store, a schoolhouse, ice-house, sawmill, harness shop, blacksmith, corn cribs, and other assorted buildings. Jim had just recently acquired the original post office from a nearby town and was working on it; the interior gutted, the roof protected by a tarp, but the original façade well on its way toward restoration.

Jim met up with us at the schoolhouse. He swept the snow from the threshold with his boot and we entered. Amazing; Jim not only rebuilt the buildings but furnished them inside as though they were still in use. The little schoolhouse was divided into two rooms. In one was an old desk and chair, along with some old books. In the other were several old-fashioned school desks, a chalkboard, and everything else that a nineteenth-century student would need.

Jim said that he often has school groups and historical societies dropping by to visit, as well as other visitors. In warmer months, visitors can buy organic produce, and there are often craftspeople and musicians on hand.

But this was January and we were all freezing out there in the snow, so Jim suggested we move inside. Entering the cozy farmhouse in which Jim lives I was immediately wrapped in welcoming warmth from the wood-burning stove in the corner. The pungent—and somehow nostalgic— aroma of wood smoke filled the house. Kicking off our wet shoes, Sonya and I sat on the couch while Jim poured us all big mugs of hot tea.

The farmhouse was a hybrid, Jim explained. The front room in which we now sat was about 170 years old and had the notorious reputation of being the site of the last murder in

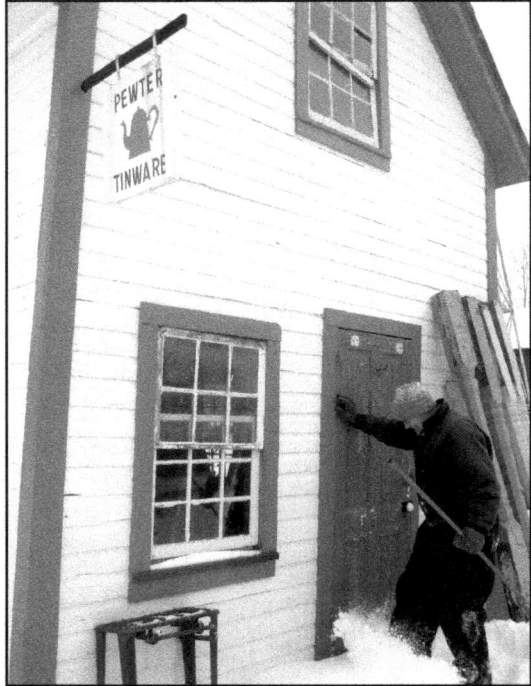

Jim Fry of Stone Garden Farm

Summit County; a jilted lover returned to avenge himself on his former girlfriend but shot and killed her mother instead. He later hanged for the crime. The back part of the house, containing the kitchen, was only a few decades younger than the front room. Jim had "hijacked" it from another farm and attached it to the other part.

The farm was interesting, as were Jim's preservation efforts, but I was looking for a ghost story. Was there one?

Jim assured me there was, although he didn't care for the word "ghost."

"Sometimes you see people without bodies because you're supposed to," Jim said. "They're a lot like us, just people that are *lighter*. They're living their lives, just doing their thing, just in a different form. Sometimes you just see them by accident."

"And you've seen them," I said.

"Tell him about Mrs. Garman," Sonya interjected.

Jim said that Howard and Julie Garman used to own the adjacent farm. He could remember visiting her when he was a boy; at that time she was already about 100 years old. Many years after she had passed away, Jim was busy working on one of the buildings he was reconstructing.

"I was pulling nails out of the floor," Jim said. "For whatever reason, I turned around quickly and there was Mrs. Garman, not as I knew her, but I saw her as she was when she was young. She was tall and small-waisted. She wore a chocolate brown dress with white lace at the sleeves and a white lace collar. Her hair was done up in an old-fashioned bun."

"What did you do?" I asked.

"Nothing. She smiled at me and nodded her head 'yes.' I took that to mean that she approved of the work I was doing. Then she disappeared."

"Have there been other ghosts?" I asked. I had the suspicion that, with all the old buildings Jim was bringing to his farm, he might also be bringing old ghosts that had some attachments to them.

"Once I saw a woman looking down at me from an upstairs window as I came to the house," Sonya said. "There was no one here except Jim."

Jim nodded. "I'm completely open to it." He went on to explain that he had spent a great deal of time with various Native American elders and holy people and that they had taught him much of their traditional wisdom. He believed that could be a reason why so many spirits gravitate toward the farm. "Because of that there are a number of Native American people here in spirit," Jim said. "This is a nice place for spirits to pass through."

Jim told us about the time he had visited the Little Big Horn Battlefield in Montana where in 1876 Sioux, Cheyenne, and

Arapaho warriors annihilated Ohio-born Gen. George Armstrong Custer's force of 263 soldiers. There were Native Americans from several tribes at the battlefield the day Jim visited, including some Crow friends of his. The Crow said that they could hear the spirits of Custer's dead soldiers crying. Jim felt pity for the soldiers. He walked from one grave to the next, inviting each soldier ghost to follow him. Then, he began a ceremony designed to free the poor spirits, to allow them to find their way to wherever it is we go after we die. He was interrupted, though, and unable to complete the ceremony, although he believed he had sent all the ghosts on their way.

Immediately after his trip to Little Big Horn, Jim visited a tribal elder on the Seneca reservation in upstate New York. When he returned to Ohio, the elder called him on the phone and asked him why she had all these soldier ghosts walking around in her house, crying. Jim explained what had happened at the battlefield. Apparently, some of the soldiers had been from New York and so returned home with him. The Seneca elder performed a ceremony that freed those trapped spirits as well.

In addition to Native American ghosts, Jim has seen animal spirits roaming through the farm, most notably wolves and white buffaloes.

On the fourth Sunday of each month Jim conducts a "dowsers' meeting" at his farmhouse. The agenda, though, is broader than dowsing—an ancient tool now being used by many ghost-hunters—and invariably touches on various paranormal topics. Jim is an open and welcoming kind of guy so attending one of these meetings might be a good way to get in touch with the ghosts of Stone Garden Farm.

Spotlight On: O.P.I.N.

In 1996 Brian Parsons founded the Ohio Paranormal Investigation Network (O.P.I.N.). The group is located in Northfield, Ohio, and has members from the Cleveland and Akron areas. O.P.I.N. focuses on client-centered investigations (coaching and empowering clients through their situation) while also investigating popular ghosthunt sites. O.P.I.N.'s mission is to educate the public, one person at a time; helping clients understand their situation while guiding them through it, helping ghosts and spirits when possible; maintaining a positive reflection of the paranormal field to the general public; and educating the public about the reality of what ghosthunters do and how it is different from the popular images portrayed on paranormal based television shows.

Each member of the group has his own favorite location to investigate, from Waverly Hills and Mansfield Reformatory to the Knickerbocker Hotel in Linesville, Pennsylvania. Brian's favorite haunt is Punderson Manor in Newbury, Ohio (see the chapter on Punderson in this book). The location is a beautiful and historic English Tudor mansion. Its paranormal history was thoroughly documented in the late 1970s and early 1980s by the late paranormal investigator Robert Van Der Velde. Many guests still report strange encounters during their visits there.

Spotlight On:
The Haunted Housewife

Theresa Argie may bill herself humorously as "The Haunted Housewife," but she is also one of the most methodical, knowledgeable, and objective paranormal investigators I know. I have had the pleasure of working with her at Punderson Manor (see the Punderson Manor chapter in this book) and other locations and have always been impressed by her careful preparations and her professional manner.

Theresa is a member of Paranormal Researchers of Ohio (PRO), "a Christian-based organization, located in Northeast Ohio, dedicated to the research and investigation of paranormal activities, as well as educating the public about ghosts and the field of the paranormal. We research claims of hauntings and ghost sightings, assist other paranormal agencies with their investigations and research, and perform cleansings (smudging) as well as Christian House Blessings."

Theresa readily admits that it's not easy to prove the existence of ghosts, but proof matters little to the family that believes their house is haunted. "Answers may be more important than proof," Theresa says. "If I tell someone, after spending seven hours in their house, that yes, their house is haunted, how am I helping them? They already know that. That's why they called me. Now what do they do? They don't want a label. They are searching for peace of mind, an explanation, answers to their questions, a way to ease their fears. I think we have to take it on faith and just keep searching. It's the journey that I find so compelling. "

In addition to her work with PRO, Theresa has worked with other paranormal investigators, including myself, and also conducted a "Ghosthunting 101" class at the haunted Olde School House in Mayfield Village, Ohio.

As seriously as she takes her work, however, her sense of humor often comes through, a tool I highly recommend for all ghosthunters. She says, "I've had to explain to my in-laws that the camcorders set up in the bedroom are not for what they are thinking. And why I have volumes of photo albums filled with pictures of dark empty rooms. Why, when my children think the boogeyman is hiding in the closet, they run for their cameras and digital recorders instead of the 'monster spray.' Or, why I want to spend family vacations in Gettysburg, not Disney World. This is the norm at my house. I am a paranormal investigator."

That sense of humor was put on display in April 2010 when Theresa and her police officer husband, Jay, appeared on Jerry Seinfeld's TV program *The Marriage Ref.* Their issue? How Theresa's passion for ghosthunting affects her other roles of wife and mother of three children.

Spotlight On:
The Real Ghost Whisperer

Most people do not know that the popular TV show *Ghost Whisperer* is based upon the real-life experiences of Mary Ann Winkowski, a North Royalton native. Mary Ann is friendly and funny, a down-to-earth Midwesterner, not at all what you would expect from one who has had the ability to see dead people since she was three years old. Over the years, I have gotten to know Mary Ann and each time I meet her, I am amazed once again by yet another of her eerie stories.

It was Mary Ann's Italian grandmother who discovered that her granddaughter had the ability to see the recently departed, and so she started bringing little Mary Ann to funerals where the girl would give the grieving family a message from their dead loved one. By the time she was seven years old, her grandmother would take her to people's houses to clear them of ghosts. Her abilities grew as she matured and today, Mary Ann not only is consulted by grieving families but is also in demand by various law enforcement agencies and people who believe that they have ghosts in their homes.

Mary Ann had already developed a local reputation as a psychic or medium—although she would not use those terms to speak about herself—when she met the famous psychic James Van Praagh, who introduced her to some TV producers. The result was *Ghost Whisperer*, starring Jennifer Love Hewitt, with Mary Ann serving as a consultant.

Mary Ann has a much different view of ghosts than what is typically portrayed in movies and on TV. "You don't walk through a ghost," she says. "You can't sit on a ghost, a ghost is not bloody-gory, ghosts don't puke, ghosts don't bleed. The ones that I see, I see identically as if I was looking at you — hair color, eye color, the clothes you have on. The only difference is, if I squinted, I could

probably see through
them."

It's not easy being
able to see and speak
to the dead. Mary Ann
says that once the
dead discover that she
can communicate with
them, they won't leave
her alone, pestering her
about some concern of
theirs until she gives
in and helps them out.
Once she does, she is
able to help the dead
"cross over" to where

Mary Ann Winkowski
www.maryannghostbuster.com

they belong. At that point, she is no longer able to communicate
with them.

In addition to her work, Mary Ann makes many public
appearances and is the author of *When the Ghost Speaks*.

Ghosts of the Ashtabula Train Disaster

ASHTABULA

ON THE EVENING OF DECEMBER 29, 1876, the No. 5 "Pacific Express" train crept toward the village of Ashtabula, inching its way along the tracks in a blinding snowstorm. Three feet of snow had already fallen, and temperatures hovered at around ten degrees below zero. A forty-mile-per-hour wind whipped the snow into huge drifts.

Approximately 197 passengers and crew huddled in the thirteen-car train, warmed by stoves in each car and illuminated by cozy oil lamps. Two engines, Socrates and Columbia, labored through the snowdrifts as the train approached the wrought-iron bridge spanning the icy waters of Ashtabula Creek seventy feet below. Inside the train, some of the ladies and children had already retired to their sleeping berths while some of the men played a last hand of cards or smoked a final cigar before turning in for the evening.

Suddenly, a loud crack split the air, and the train wheels stopped moving. Engineer Dan McGuire, in the lead engine, looked back and saw Columbia sinking backwards. McGuire realized instantly that the bridge was giving way. He fired up Socrates and the engine shot forward just as the coupling between the two engines broke and Columbia disappeared.

The entire span of the bridge collapsed into the gorge below, taking with it the rest of the train. A tremendous crash came up from the creek as the cars crashed upon each other, piling up in the frigid water and swirling snow. Then, an eerie silence, but only for a few moments as the screams of the injured and dying carried above the sound of the howling wind.

Many of the passengers—the lucky ones—died immediately upon impact. Others were not as fortunate. Survivors began to struggle out through the broken windows and holes in the roofs, but less than ten minutes after the crash, fire broke out in the wreckage and quickly engulfed all the cars. Some people, caught far below the rubble, drowned in the icy waters. Others, trapped in the wreckage, died in agonizing, painful ways as the fire roasted them to death. Even some who escaped the train did not survive; blinded by the snow, they fell through the ice and drowned in the creek.

Rescue efforts were ineffectual. There was no road down to the creek bed, only some steps now buried in deep snow. Still, local residents managed to find their way down into the gorge. It took firefighters almost forty-five minutes to reach the site. Inexplicably, when they arrived at the site, they made no move to put out the fire despite the fact that at least one fire department pumper had made it to the scene. Rescuers tried using buckets of water to fight the fire, but to no avail. Pandemonium reigned; there was no organized, concerted effort to extinguish the blaze or to employ rescue operations. While there were individual instances of heroism in rescuing passengers, there were also thieves who mercilessly pilfered the bodies of the dead and injured.

The fire began to burn itself out, revealing a hellish scene. Writer Darrell E. Hamilton described it this way: "The dead lay in every direction amid the driving snow. A skull lay by itself amid a blackened heap, whitened by the fire. Other bodies lay with their eyes burned out of their skulls. Heaps of bodies, mostly women and children, lying in the sleeping coaches were still burning. The delicate form of a mother lay beside her little child. Both were reduced to mere black lumps that scarcely resembled human form. Arms, legs, and skulls lay strewn amidst the wreckage. Other bodies lay completely cut in half with no sign of the other half."

By midnight most of the survivors had been brought up from the gorge. In the cover of night thieves continued their gruesome looting of the corpses, taking all their valuables: jewelry, money, watches, even articles of clothing and unused train tickets. The next morning presented a macabre scene. The wooden train cars were reduced completely to ash, only the metal wheels and carriages remaining. Bodies and body parts lay buried in the snow and beneath the water. In the smoldering debris of the train, calcined bones and piles of white ash were all that remained of the passengers burned to death in the fire.

Because of the condition of the corpses and the lack of identification caused by the looting, it is difficult to say how many people died in the wreck. Estimates range from ninety-two to 160. Many of the bodies were claimed by relatives, but at least twenty-nine unidentified bodies were buried in a mass grave in Ashtabula's Chestnut Grove Cemetery about three weeks after the accident.

It is in Chestnut Grove Cemetery that the ghosts of the train wreck victims are most often reported. Specters wearing old-fashioned warm weather clothing, some of them carrying baskets and carpetbags, are seen walking about the tall granite obelisk that marks the mass grave. Screams sometimes echo at night in the cemetery and a rank, burning odor—like burnt human flesh—is detected in the night air.

Close by the memorial is the Gothic mausoleum of Charles Collins, the luckless railroad inspector who had missed the flaws in the bridge that contributed to its collapse. That night, standing in freezing waist-high water, he had heroically helped rescue passengers from the wreck, no doubt wracked by guilt and remorse. After testifying at an inquest into the accident, Collins went home and to bed. In the morning, a friend found him in bed dead, shot through the head. What at first seemed to be a simple case of suicide committed by a man distraught over the role he played in the accident turned out to be murder. According to the coroner's report, the situation of the body and the placement of the wounds would have made it impossible for them to have been self-inflicted. Whether suicide or murder the ghost of Charles Collins is also said to haunt Chestnut Grove Cemetery, weeping for the deaths he inadvertently caused.

The Ashtabula Creek still flows quietly through the gorge, but people say that on the anniversary of the great train disaster unearthly cries and screams echo over the dark waters.

Southeast

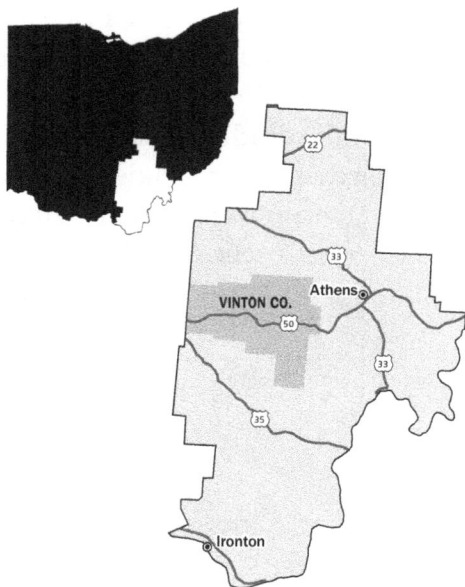

Athens
The Ridges

Ironton
Briggs-Lawrence County Public Library

Somewhere in Southeast Ohio
Mystery Farmhouse

Vinton County
Moonville Tunnel

CHAPTER 23

The Ridges
ATHENS

THERE ARE MANY SPOOKY STORIES about Athens, Ohio, a place the British Society for Psychical Research recognizes as one of the most haunted places in the world and a community profiled on Fox Family Channel's *World's Scariest Places.* Modern psychic researchers believe that the Athens area contains an extremely active vortex—that is, a portal between our world and the spirit world that allows spirits to easily travel between these realms. The Shawnee and ancient Native peoples before them knew the area as a center of strong energy, a place in which the spirits dwelt. For centuries, Native shamans and healers sought guidance and inspiration from the spirits here, especially those atop Mount Nebo, the highest peak in the region, just over 1,000 feet high. In the nineteenth century, an internationally renowned Spiritualist center was located upon Mount Nebo until lightning—considered an act of God by some pious community members—burned it to the ground.

The twin Victorian towers of The Ridges rise above the trees on a bluff overlooking the Hocking River. The Ridges is the popular name given to the sprawling institution that was founded as the Athens Lunatic Asylum in 1874 and is now owned by Ohio University. At its peak in 1953, the asylum sheltered 1,749 patients and was made up of 78 buildings spread over more than 1,000 acres. The hospital was mostly self-sufficient and had its own dairy, greenhouses, gardens, vineyards, and even a piggery.

Now it has ghosts.

The story most often told about The Ridges concerns the eerie figure of a woman imprinted upon the floor in one of the old abandoned wards, a woman who died there in 1978 under tragic and weird circumstances.

In the 1970s, the institution was known as the Athens Mental Health and Retardation Center and reflected the many advances in mental health care that had come about since the hospital's founding one hundred years before. As a result of these advances, including new pharmaceuticals that allowed many patients to function in society, the huge buildings began to empty out. Many wards stood empty and abandoned.

On December 1, 1978, a 54-year-old patient who had the privilege of leaving the grounds as long as she returned in the evening went missing. After an intensive three-day hunt and a weeklong follow-up search, the woman had not turned up. Six weeks later, a maintenance man found the woman's body in a sunlit room on an abandoned third-floor ward. She was lying naked on the cement floor beneath tall windows, arms crossed and legs composed as if she had deliberately settled herself in that posture. Some accounts say that her clothes were found neatly folded in a pile on the window sill, others that she had dropped her clothes piece by piece out the window in an attempt to attract attention to her predicament, which was that she had become accidentally locked inside the abandoned ward. The coroner listed the cause of death as heart failure.

The woman's death is strange, but what is even stranger is the impression she left upon the floor. When her body was removed, a stain was left behind that clearly depicts her body. It is believed to have been created by the interaction of her own bodily chemicals with the bright sunlight that streamed through the windows during the weeks that she remained undiscovered. Maintenance workers say that trying to scrub the stain out of the cement only darkens it.

I had heard ridiculous tales of a curse attached to anyone who dared to touch the woman's image, including the story of an Ohio University co-ed who hung herself in her dorm after touching the figure. A newspaper reporter broke the news of her death to the astonished co-ed during an interview a few years after her supposed suicide. Despite the silly stories about the unfortunate patient, I snapped a photo of her image during a nocturnal ghost investigation at The Ridges conducted by the Ohio Exploration Society.

The ghosthunters had been invited to The Ridges by Barrett Skrypeck, a fine arts graduate student and teaching associate at Ohio University. I first met Barrett when I was living in Athens and teaching writing courses at the university. I had sent an e-mail to the university's fine arts department, looking for artists to convert my rusted-out 1987 Buick Skyhawk into a

Ghosthuntermobile. Such a car would be a unique way to adver-
tise my books, I thought, and I wasn't risking much with my
old clunker. Barrett and a team of a half-dozen or so fine arts
grad students went to work on the car and painted it all over
with ghosts, demons, gravestones, haunted houses, and other
assorted paranormal symbols.

The grad students' studios were located on an upper floor
of The Ridges, in what had been one of the hospital wards. The
university could not afford to renovate the floor so maintenance
men simply moved the hospital furniture out and let the artists
in. Reminders of the patients who had once lived there were
everywhere, especially in the religious and profane graffiti they
had scratched into the exterior windowsills as they gazed out at
the world, wishing for wings. Barrett's studio, like most of the
others, was a cramped, airless space that had been a patient's
room. His artwork covered the walls, and every available inch of
surface area was filled with art supplies.

Barrett had called the Ohio Exploration Society because of
the ghosts roaming the decrepit halls of The Ridges.

"Several times, I've been sitting in my studio and, out of the
corner of my eye, I'll see a figure glide past the door," Barrett
told me. "When I get up to see who it is, no one is there."

The final-straw ghost for Barrett was the one he saw in the
men's room. As he entered the lavatory he saw a man in a black
coat and hat reflected in the long mirror above the sinks. The
position of the image in the mirror indicated that the man was
already in the restroom, but when Barrett entered, he found
himself alone. The man could not have left the room without
Barrett's knowledge since there was only one door and Barrett
had just come in through it.

"I got the hell out of there quick," Barrett said.

As you can imagine, I accepted Barrett's invitation to join
the investigation in a heartbeat.

I arrived early at The Ridges the night of the investigation. Standing outside the locked doors, I looked up and saw the lights on in the tower windows where the studios were located. Against the night sky the shadowed turrets with their lighted windows looked like something out of an old Dracula movie. The Ridges is an isolated complex, cut off from the rest of the university by the river and the high ridge itself, so the parking lot was empty, except for my Ghosthuntermobile. It was a moonless night and if anyone, or anything, was waiting in the shadows beneath the towers, I couldn't tell.

After a few minutes, a car pulled up and three men and a woman got out and approached me. This was the Ohio Exploration Society, headed by Jason Robinson. The other investigators were Jason Colwell, Misty Jones, and Abraham Bartlett. They were all, I guessed, in their mid to late twenties and had driven down from Columbus. I was particularly pleased when they showed me the copy of *Ghosthunting Ohio* that they had in the car and had been reading on their way to Athens. Since they didn't know I would be at the investigation, they weren't simply trying to impress me by reading my book; I loved these guys.

Bartlett arrived, along with his wife, Becky, and Howie (real name withheld by request) from the university's maintenance department, who would act as something of a guide for our group and would unlock doors that weren't supposed to be unlocked. We all headed upstairs to the artists' studios.

The OES crew, each of them wearing shirts emblazoned with the group's name and logo, assembled their equipment on a table in an area the students had set up as a makeshift lounge. The room was done up in a Modern Goodwill motif and furnished with hideous orange upholstered chairs oozing their stuffing out of various rips and tears, a battered old TV, a small bookcase, and a weird assortment of decorative items hanging on the walls, including a collection of different-colored teddy

bears and the naked torso of a doll whose face had been gar-
ishly painted à la KISS's Gene Simmons and whose chest bore a
crude pentacle. Artists, I thought, go figure.

The lounge was situated in one of the building's towers and
it was through its long narrow windows that I had seen the light
from down below. Unlike the rest of us, Howie was an Athens
native and had actually known some of the patients who were
housed in the building when it was in use as a hospital. He was
decked out in a ball cap, denim jacket, and jeans with a silver
belt buckle the size of a dinner plate.

"This area right here," he said, "used to be the patients' day
room. You could see them looking out the windows, just wandering around here. I knew one of them, a family friend, maybe
a distant relative, I'm not sure, named Hazel. My family used to
visit her and I'd come along."

Howie walked over to the window and stood looking out at
the parking lot down below, washed in yellow light from a single
lamppost. He jingled the large ring of keys he wore on his belt
and then turned back to us.

"Hazel died several years ago, but she's never left this building. I know. I've seen her. Sometimes I'd be working outside
and I'll look up and there she is, big as life, standing behind the
windows, watching me."

"How do you know it was Hazel and not one of the artists?"
I asked.

"Well, first, because I knew her. I know what she looks like.
Second, she was a different lady. Large. Red hair. She stood out
in a crowd."

"Did you ever see her inside the building?"

"Yes," Howie said, "I saw her standing in the doorway to
what used to be the patients' activities room, wearing a yellow
dress. There's plenty going on here, I'll tell you. Late at night, I'll
be here by myself and I'll hear doors opening and closing, foot-

steps, that kind of thing. And I don't drink on the job," Howie added, even though I hadn't asked.

The OES investigators had unpacked their equipment and had laid it all out on the table. Jason Robinson explained to me how his group would conduct its investigation. A tall, thin guy wearing an OES T-shirt and navy ball cap turned backwards, Jason held a video camcorder in his hand while he spoke.

"First, we'll walk through the building and get an idea of its layout. We especially want to see the areas where people have reported something happening. Then we'll set up a few cameras on tripods in those areas and run tape for a while, see what happens. We'll also leave some recorders in other areas and see if we can pick up any EVPs." I knew that EVPs were electronic voice phenomena, recordings of voices, supposedly spirit voices that were captured on the recorders although inaudible to the people in the room at that time. "Every so often, we'll go around and check out the equipment, make sure everything is running right," Jason said.

As we stood talking, I noticed that more people were congregating in the lounge. Some of the other artists whose studios were in the building had joined us, accompanied by friends they had invited along. There were close to two-dozen people now. Some of them were sipping beer, a commodity easily found among the artists. The investigation was rapidly taking on the complexion of a frat party.

"A lot of people," I said to Jason. "Will that affect your investigation?"

He frowned. "It might, but it's a big building. Maybe if we split up, it might work out better."

It seemed, however, that everyone wanted to go along on the initial tour led by Howie. I couldn't blame them since the abandoned wards of the hospital were off-limits to the public because of safety concerns, yet were the source of much local speculation about ghosts. There was no way, however, that any respectable ghost would put in an appearance as this rowdy, beer-swilling circus tromped through the dark and dusty halls.

The OES team, to their credit, remained aloof to the shenanigans of the others and tried their best to conduct a serious investigation. For my part, whenever Howie led us into yet another gloomy hall, I separated myself from the others as best I could in order to soak up in solitude as much of the environment as possible. This had been my modus operandi in countless other visits to haunted locations, simply to find a quiet place where I could be alone, open, and receptive to whatever may reside in that place. It wasn't easy to employ that method that night, but I tried.

I wandered in and out of dark rooms without a flashlight and wondered what had taken place in them. Had they been patients' rooms? Were they treatment rooms? Nurses' stations? Most of the furnishings were long gone, but every so often, I would stumble across an old chair, cabinet, or other small piece of furniture. I could hear the others walking in the hall, sometimes see the beams of their flashlights bouncing over the floor, as I stood quietly in a room, waiting. No positive emotions emanated from that place. Locked in their dementia, these poor patients had suffered. Hundreds of them lay buried in two cemeteries on the hospital's grounds, many of them beneath stone markers that bore only a number. The reason for this anonymity seems to have been to spare family members the indignity and embarrassment of publicly revealing that a relative had been committed to the Lunatic Asylum. It was sad to think that these people, who suffered in life through no fault of their own and endured horrific "treatments" in an attempt to cure them of their maladies, would lie beneath the green grass still spurned by humanity. If ever there were a place where lost souls clamored for recognition, for dignity, for peace, it was those cemeteries.

I could hear the voices of the others growing fainter, so I trailed behind them as Howie led us all up a flight of stairs to the ward in which the woman had died in 1978. We entered the small room where the body had been found, and I wondered once again how it was that she was unable to make her presence known through the tall windows to rescuers outside. The thought struck me that perhaps she wasn't looking to be saved. Maybe it was simply her time to die and she knew it. Accepted it. Flashlights played across her image, still clearly visible upon the dusty concrete floor; the OES team shot some video and still photography.

Howie took us up to the attic. The space below the sloping roof of the building was enormous and was divided into several large rooms, separated by brick walls. Arched doorways led from one room into another. Oddly, the floor was covered with a layer of soft dirt rather than dust, and none of us, Howie included, could account for its origin. We wandered around in the attic, poking into nooks and little rooms. The wiring and ductwork typical of an institutional building snaked through the attic, but there was nothing else up there. Jason's flashlight did find evidence that someone had discovered the attic a long time ago. As he entered another long room, the light picked up some graffiti spray-painted on the brick wall in two-foot-high letters. The graffiti read: *July 11.1960 Kennedy for President.* I had been only ten years old when some unknown Democrat painted the slogan in the attic. Where no one would ever see it.

From the attic we walked all the way down to the basement, a dark and dirty warren of rooms and tunnels. After so much trekking through the building, the most boisterous of the group were starting to lag and some had broken off from the group to find their way back to the comfort of the artists' lounge and, presumably, more beer. The remainder of us explored the basement, probing through piles of old junk, including sections of the hospital's original wrought-iron fences and gates. In a tiny brick room Howie showed us a cistern in which he said one of the doctors had kept a pet alligator. Howie didn't know why.

We emerged from the basement and went back upstairs to the artists' studios. There, the OES team decided where they would place their cameras and audio recorders. They set up a video camera on a tripod in a section of abandoned offices, and another in an ominous room on the same floor as the studios, a room in which blue ceramic tiles completely covered the walls. Drains were set in the floor. Metal jets protruded from the walls, maybe for gas or oxygen, no one knew. The room reminded me of an old-fashioned surgical suite, but it could just as easily have been a kitchen. A couple people in the group said that they felt some sort of "presence" in that room. Another camera and recorder were set up in the lavatory where Barrett had seen his ghost.

Then we waited. This is one aspect of ghosthunting that none of the popular television programs about ghosthunters ever seem to show—the boring wait for something to happen. Often, nothing does happen. Ghosthunters live for the momentary glimpse of something unusual on a video monitor, or for a few seconds of unidentifiable sound on a recording, and it can take many hours of investigation to produce those few results. Ghosts don't respond well to command performances and are notorious for making themselves known when all the cameras, recorders, and other monitoring equipment are already turned off or removed. Still, it is quite a rush when something does make itself known.

Every now and then, Jason or one of the members of his team would make the rounds and check the equipment. Sometimes, they would take still photos as they went. I accompanied Jason and Abe Bartlett on one such check. I asked them how often they had encountered ghosts on their investigations and, while they admitted that it was pretty unusual to actually see an apparition, they had collected a good number of EVPs from some of the places they had investigated. Although a relatively new group, the Ohio Exploration Society had already conducted investigations into dozens of haunted cemeteries, houses, hospitals, restaurants, Native American burial mounds (fairly common in Ohio), schools, and other assorted haunts.

Nothing unusual happened that night at The Ridges. The partygoers quickly tired of the whole thing and left, no doubt seeking the livelier haunts of the Court Street bars catering to Ohio University students. That left Barrett and Becky, Howie, a couple of die-hard artists, the OES team, and me to close down the investigation. Around 1 a.m. we packed up the equipment and called it a night.

It takes quite awhile for an investigative team to analyze the film, photos, and recordings that are made during the investigation, so it was a couple weeks before I again heard from Jason. Apparently, I had been wrong in thinking that nothing had happened that night. Although we never felt their presence, the ghosts of The Ridges certainly knew we were there and did their best to communicate with us. The OES team had recorded two EVPs. In a room that had formerly been a padded cell, Jason recorded someone yelling on his digital audio recorder. As the group came up from the basement Misty Jones's microcassette recorder picked up a chilling, whispered voice saying, *Would you help us?* The proverbial hairs on the back of my neck stood to attention when I heard that voice.

Who are these ghosts? How can they be helped? After all those poor spirits endured when they were flesh and blood, it would be a blessing if someone could reach them and set them free.

CHAPTER 24

Moonville Tunnel
VINTON COUNTY

LIKE MOST OF RURAL SOUTHEAST OHIO, Vinton County is densely wooded and sparsely populated, much of the county being taken up by Zaleski State Forest. Mysteries abide in the hilly terrain, deep woods, and abandoned mines of the area. It is here that the Grassman, Ohio's version of Bigfoot, reportedly stalks the woods and it is here that ghosts float in the darkness of the Moonville Tunnel.

Moonville is a ghost town. The only remains of the tiny little mining community that peaked in the 1870s are the half-buried foundations of some houses, a little hilltop cemetery, and the old Marietta and Cincinnati Railroad tunnel itself. The train tracks were torn up years ago and the trestle bridge crossing Raccoon

Creek demolished, but none of that keeps the ghosts from making their endless nocturnal rounds.

In its early days most of the residents of Moonville worked at the nearby Hope Furnace. During the Civil War, when the Hope Furnace and other local furnaces began turning out tons of iron to be used for Union army weapons and artillery, the residents of Moonville found work in the coal mines, hauling out the precious fuel to keep the furnaces running day and night. Despite the dangers inherent in mining, the ghosts of Moonville have nothing to do with the mines but are, instead, associated with the railroad that once passed through the little village.

One of the most dangerous jobs on nineteenth-century trains was that of brakeman. To do the job correctly required strength, agility, alertness, and timing. One false move could injure or kill a brakeman. An 1877 edition of *Harper's Weekly* contained a drawing of a brakeman working atop a railroad car in a snowstorm. The caption read: "THE FREIGHT-TRAIN BRAKEMAN. The position of a freight-train brakeman is one of peculiar hardship and peril, especially in winter, when he must stand, without shelter, exposed to wind, rain, or snow, ready to obey the sharp warning of the engineer's whistle. For this duty young men of hardy frame, strong nerve, and steady habits are selected; for it requires all these qualities to perform the duties of the post. No one whose nerves are unstrung by drinking could be trusted where a slip of hand or foot, or unsteadiness of sight, might plunge him headlong to destruction. Our sketch, true to life, gives a graphic idea of what he must endure on a stormy winter night, when the brake handles chill through his heavy gloves, and the steps and car roofs are as slippery as the surface of a skating rink."

The most famous Moonville ghost is that of a brakeman who was killed by a train on which he was working. People see his lantern swinging to and fro and advancing toward them in the darkness of Moonville Tunnel.

There is plenty of documentation to support the existence of this ghost. A March 31, 1859, article in the McArthur, Ohio, *Democrat* reported: "A brakesman on the Marietta & Cincinnati Railroad fell from the cars near Cincinnati Furnace, on last Tuesday March 29, 1859, and was fatally injured, when the wheels passing over and grinding to a shapeless mass the greater part of one of his legs. He was taken on the train to Hamden and Doctors Wolf and Rannells sent for to perform amputation, but the prostration of the vital energies was too great to attempt it. The man is probably dead ere this. The accident resulted from a too free use of liquor."

Less than twenty years later, this article appeared in the *Athens Messenger* on July 17, 1873: "A brakeman . . . named McDevitt was caught between two colliding platforms and had both legs and one arm horribly mangled . . . McDevitt survived his injuries only a short time. The deceased we learn was about 21 years of age, and leaves a widowed mother."

In 1876 Michael Marboro was killed while working on the Cincinnati and Marietta line and eight years later, his brother Thomas, was also killed.

It is unclear which one of these unfortunate railroad workers is the ghost that haunts the tunnel. Perhaps they all haunt the tunnel, working in shifts. No matter; the many people who have witnessed the ghostly light know that *someone* long dead continues to stalk the tunnel.

In 1993 a student from Ohio University in nearby Athens went for a swim with three friends in Raccoon Creek. On the way back, they headed through the tunnel, two of them walking ahead of the others. Shortly after entering the tunnel the two students in the lead came running back to the others saying that they had seen a light moving in the tunnel seemingly all by itself floating in air. One of the other students went to investigate. He was quoted in an *Athens Messenger* news story as saying, "It was just a swinging light with no one holding it. I hightailed it back to the car. I haven't been back out there since."

There are other ghosts, though, connected to the Moonville Tunnel. One of them, a man, is often seen standing still atop the tunnel. It is reported that he sometimes throws rocks at people walking below.

This ghost is believed to be that of David "Baldie" Keeton, a frequent drunk who was enjoying himself one night in 1886 at the Hope-Moonville saloon. Keeton was a barroom brawler and, true to form, got into a fight with a man named Jim Mace that night. Mace finally got Keeton in a headlock and would have broken his neck had not the saloon keeper put an end to the fight. He threw Keeton out of the saloon, warning him to leave town "or else." Staggering his way home from the saloon, unknown assailants jumped him near the tunnel and murdered him. No one was ever apprehended for the crime.

Although a rock-throwing ghost is not a good thing, we should be grateful that Keeton's ghost doesn't come down from the tunnel looking for a fight; in life he was known to squeeze the life out of a man with his ferocious "bear-hugs."

The remaining two ghosts of Moonville Tunnel are women, both of them struck and killed by trains. In 1873 an unidentified woman from the mining town of Mineral was walking along the trestle crossing Raccoon Creek when she was hit by the morning express train. In 1905 Mrs. Patrick Shea, a woman in her eighties, was walking from Moonville to Hope and was struck by a train while crossing the trestle. One of her legs required amputation and she died from shock.

Most people think it is the unidentified woman that still walks the area in which her broken body was found after being hit by the train. Some people claim to detect the scent of lavender on the breeze, the same scent often used in old-fashioned ladies' fragrances. One witness to the woman's ghost said that the spirit followed him along the tracks. Panicked, he broke into a run but the ghost kept right up with him until he veered off the tracks and the ghost vanished.

Visitors to Moonville Tunnel no longer have to worry about being struck by a train since the tracks were torn up more than twenty years ago. But with the removal of the trestle, crossing Raccoon Creek can be tricky, especially when the creek waters are running high. The creek bank is steep in places, but with a little patience, ghosthunters can make it to the other side without turning themselves into ghosts.

Spotlight On: Hope Furnace

The little mining community of Hope in Vinton County no longer exists, its ruins submerged below the waters of manmade Lake Hope. But the nineteenth-century iron furnace that once employed most of Hope's residents, either as furnace workers or as miners extracting coal necessary for its operation, still exists.

During the Civil War the Hope Furnace operated night and day, its hellish glow shining in the darkness, as tons of iron came pouring forth to be turned into weapons and artillery for the Union Army. It might be from the war years that the ghost story associated with the furnace comes to us.

In 1863 Gen. John Hunt Morgan led his Confederate troops on a raid through southern Ohio, posing a threat to Cincinnati and

Spotlight On: Hope Furnace
(continued)

then striking east across the state before finally being captured near the West Virginia border. No doubt, Morgan and his raiders would have been happy if they had been able to destroy any of the sixty-nine ironworks in southeastern Ohio's Hanging Rock iron region, at that time one of the most productive iron-producing areas in the world. With Morgan's raiders roaming the countryside, guards were posted at the ironworks and the Confederate plans to attack the works thwarted.

The stone, pyramidal Hope Furnace backs up to a ridge, and it is believed that one stormy night, with the threat of Morgan's raiders in the air, a guard at the ironworks paced the ridge, peering through the wind and the rain, keeping alert for any sign of the Confederates. On the muddy, slippery ridge the guard lost his footing and fell into the chimney of the furnace. His unheard screams would have been short-lived as his body would have melted away in minutes. Smokin' Joe, as the unidentified ghost is nicknamed, remains at his post to this day. Nocturnal visitors to the site have seen his silhouette and lantern moving along the ridge. More curiously, one ghosthunter group climbed inside the furnace—despite the iron grate covering the entrance—and recorded an EVP. They heard Smokin' Joe say, *I am right here*, followed by, *Cold!*

Odd, isn't it? One would think Smokin' Joe would be plenty warm.

CHAPTER 25

Mystery Farmhouse
SOMEWHERE IN SOUTHEAST OHIO

IT WAS DUSK ON AN UNSEASONABLY WARM Friday the thirteenth as Sherri Brake and I bumped up the gravel road in Sherri's black Toyota 4Runner. I was riding shotgun. Through the windshield I could see the daylight quickly fading behind the old blue farmhouse that squatted on a patch of lawn surrounded by fields left fallow. A handful of shaggy pine trees fringed the house.

"This is it," Sherri said, as she turned the Toyota onto the lawn. "I wonder if anyone is here yet."

"The lights are on inside," I said, leaning over the front seat.

We got out of the truck.

There was a pickup truck parked alongside a small outbuilding. Behind it stood a lone rusted silo, the top missing. I noticed dark clouds suddenly descending upon the forested hillsides in the distance and felt a cold breeze spring up. A flash of lightning sliced through the gathering gloom. Thunder grumbled over the fields. A few drops of rain fell. Appropriate for Friday the thirteenth, I thought.

"Let's see if we can beat the rain," Sherri said. She opened the back of the truck to retrieve her equipment.

I didn't move.

As I stood there watching the storm swarm up over the hills, a towering figure came lumbering from around back of the outbuilding. A bear, I thought, but no, the figure was human. The guy stood six feet tall. He wore muddy work boots, jeans with suspenders, and an electric blue t-shirt that could not prevent his belly from hanging over his belt. He came closer, revealing a gray Willie Nelson beard and blue and white bandana tied around a head of thinning hair.

He carried a rifle.

"We're dead," I said.

But the man didn't shoot. Instead, as the car carrying our other team members, Vince and Hannah, pulled in beside Sherri's truck, he offered to help us bring some of the gear inside the house. His name was Larry and he maintained the abandoned farmhouse for the owner. We quickly dubbed him Big Larry, since the man who had asked Sherri to come out and investigate the farmhouse was also named Larry.

I figured it was a lucky thing he didn't shoot us in the rapidly gathering dark and attributed our good luck to the bird that had defecated on my shirt only an hour before as we ate our dinner on the deck of a biker bar in town. Italian custom declares such a disgusting occasion—the bird crap, not the biker bar—to be auspicious. The cornfields of Ohio were a far cry from Italy but I'm half-Italian, so I went with it.

The rain was starting to come down harder now as we lugged the rest of our gear inside, piling it up on a table in the little parlor. Tripod, video-cam, digital cameras, tape recorders, EMF (electromagnetic frequency) meters, thermometers, flashlights, dowsing rods, and of course, chocolate chip cookies, coffee, and a cooler of cold drinks. We were prepared.

Sherri had been to the 1820s farmhouse once before, and she led the rest of us on a quick tour of the house. The room in which we gathered was small and square with a crazy-quilt pattern of at least four different kinds of wallpaper plastered over each other or peeling off the walls. Large bare patches broke up what remained of the wallpaper. In some places, the walls had rotted down to the lathing. On the wall above the table where we had dropped our gear were three shelves upon which were arranged an odd assortment of objects d'junk; ceramic dogs and frogs—a lot of frogs—shotgun shells, a baseball, a flowerpot, a little wooden car, a miniature lighthouse, and salt and pepper shakers.

To the right of this room was a parlor with the same designer wall treatment. A single bare bulb on a shadeless lamp dimly lit the room. A beat-up blue recliner and saggy couch sat on the dusty wood floor. The window on the far wall was opened to the elements. In the weak light, a long tattered curtain flapped wildly in the wind, casting dancing shadows on the wall.

In the back half of the house was the kitchen, which still contained a table, oven, and refrigerator. The ceiling here was cracked and flaking away and sagged dangerously around the lamp suspended over the table. There was a door to the outside but it was sealed over with clear plastic sheeting which was nailed to the wall. A good-luck horseshoe was hung above the door. An old summer kitchen opened off the back of the kitchen. It hadn't been used for many years and served now as a dark and dusty storage space.

A few weeks before, a skeptical friend had accompanied Sherri to the house. During their visit he saw a ghost: a grandmotherly type wearing an apron. She was standing in the doorway at the rear of the house looking at him. Then she vanished as suddenly as she had appeared.

Another empty room, perhaps a former bedroom, was located off the kitchen. Opening what I thought was a closet revealed a narrow flight of stairs to the second floor. Peering up, all I saw was darkness. Sherri and I crept up the stairs, our flashlights piercing the dark.

There were two bedrooms upstairs, both of them in bad condition. Sherri and I entered the first, at the front of the house.

"Oh man, do you feel that?" Sherri asked.

I did. As soon as we stepped into the room, I felt an oppressive heaviness in the air, almost as if I was underwater. But the feeling was not simply external. I felt uncomfortable pressure, a fullness deep within me, seated low in my belly. and I understood exactly what it meant when someone said they had "a gut feeling" about something.

"This room is really charged," Sherri said, setting a small lantern down on the floor.

A crash of thunder suddenly broke the oppressive stillness of the room. Lightning flashed outside, illuminating through the windows a line of trees being whipped by the wind. Rain pelted the roof above us. We played our lights around the room. An old carpet lay rolled up to one side of the room. In a corner, the wooden headboard of a small bed stood propped against the wall.

Then I heard the children. Muffled beneath the beating rain and rolling thunder, the sounds were indistinct at first, but as I moved closer to the headboard I could hear them more clearly.

"What is it?" Sherri said, watching me.

"Listen."

She came over to where I stood listening.

I heard high-pitched squealing and chattering, the sounds of children on a playground far away.

"What *is* that?" Sherri asked.

I shook my head and shined my light into the corner and over the headboard. "I don't know," I said. "Critters of some kind, I guess. There must be all kinds of animals in these walls. Squirrels, raccoons, mice, who knows?"

"Probably, but this room's loaded with negative energy," she said. "I'm going to set up a camera in here."

She retrieved her equipment from downstairs and set up the video recorder on the tripod in a corner of the room. We briefly checked out the rear bedroom, and then went back downstairs.

The other Larry—Little Larry—had just arrived, accompanied by a lady friend. He was the star of the show, since he had been the one to originally contact Sherri, telling her about the ghosts he had seen at the house and asking her to investigate. Little Larry was an older man, with gray hair and a thick gray moustache. He was a retired cop with thirty-five years on the force and he was still dressed like one in black shoes and pants, black jacket. A soft-spoken man, his face bore a weary expression, as if he had been kept awake for a long time and had great worries troubling him.

Sherri had told me over the phone that Little Larry's ghost stories, as strange as they seemed, were consistent in their details, no matter how often he related them. That consistency made him more credible, she thought. As he sat on a folding chair in our "headquarters," nursing a cold coffee, he once again told us what he had seen or sometimes felt.

His first ghostly experience at the house occurred when he and his dog entered into the very room where we were now gathered and Little Larry sensed the presence of several "gangsters" there. He didn't actually see them as much as sense their presence.

"I was wearing my police uniform at the time," Little Larry said, "and I could feel that the spirits hated my guts." He was certain they meant to do him harm. He left the house in a hurry.

On another visit to the house, he saw a woman, surrounded by a Christmas wreath with lighted candles, peering down at him from an upstairs window. A different time, he saw a man wearing a Civil War uniform standing in an upstairs bedroom. Little Larry also saw two children in the house. These were apparently, the same two children that Laura Wissler, a psychic friend of Sherri's, had seen in the front bedroom on Sherri's first visit there and had "released to the light," meaning that she had helped those poor ghosts find their way to peace.

Little Larry said he had researched the house and had documents "from Columbus," documents that we never saw, which verified several facts that might explain the hauntings: the house was used as a gang hangout during the Prohibition era; a previous owner who had lost a leg at Antietam during the Civil War fell out of the barn hayloft, broke his neck, and died; a man murdered his cheating wife in the front room; an Indian trading post existed on the site before the house was built, and an entire family, including thirteen children, were trapped inside the post and burned to death during an Indian raid, their bodies buried on the premises.

Little Larry had rented the house several years earlier, hoping to move in, but he never did. "I can't. They won't let me," he said, speaking of the ghosts. He and his buddy, Big Larry, now used the house as a sort of hunting cabin, but Little Larry said that he would never stay at the house by himself. This from a man who said he had seen ghosts all his life, including during his tour of duty in Vietnam.

There was still a member of our team missing. The psychic, Laura, and her husband had not yet arrived, no doubt delayed by the storm. We waited for her, listening to Little Larry's stories, now and then checking the house with the EMF meters, but getting no unusual results.

Sherri and I took a pair of dowsing rods to the bedrooms upstairs. The front bedroom still felt "heavy," although not as much as before. Using the dowsing rods I detected a spot in the room at which the rods crossed, indicating some source of energy. I walked through the spot and the rods uncrossed after a few steps. Every time I stepped back into the space, the rods crossed; when I came out, they uncrossed. I could find no apparent energy source that would have made the rods move, but I was aware of a pitch in the floor that I could not rule out as a factor in their movement. Sherri trained the EMF meter in the area without any odd results.

The rain had let up so we decided to go outside to check the grounds and the barn. The whole group wandered out into the darkness. A line of tall pine trees marked the boundary between the back lawn and the fields. The trees were spaced evenly apart and had obviously been planted there by some former owner. It was there in a line between two of the trees that Sherri detected the bodies.

Little Larry had said that the victims of the Indian attack had been buried on the grounds. It was also possible that other owners of the farm and their families had been buried on the premises as well, family burial plots being common in earlier times. Now, while I held the flashlight on her, Sherri dowsed the area beneath the trees. As she walked a line between the trees, the rods crossed at three evenly spaced spots. She mapped out three areas of energy, each about five feet long, roughly the length of a body. She handed me the rods, and I detected pretty much the same areas.

"I think there are bodies here," Sherri said, holding a single rod over one of the sites. "By their size, I would say they were young. Teenagers maybe, possibly younger than that." She turned to Little Larry. "Do you know if there were any burials in this spot?"

"Not for sure," he said. "The documents only say that people were buried on the property."

"What about the barn?" I asked. "Should we try there?"

Little Larry and his lady friend went back to sit on the porch of the house and wait for Laura. Big Larry led the rest of us through the field to the barn. Bats darted through the dark barn, caught briefly in our lights. I was still holding a pair of dowsing rods so I thought I'd give them a try in the barn. To my amazement, I found an area of energy about eight feet by five feet.

"What the heck?" I said. I looked up and saw a smile on Big Larry's face. "What?"

"You found the car," he said.

"The car?"

"He dowsed a car?" Sherri said. "What were you concentrating on?" she asked me.

"Nothing, just energy. Not a car, that's for sure. You mean there's a car buried down there?" I said to Big Larry. "Why?"

He shrugged, his shadow looming against the barn wall. "I don't know why. All I know is a previous owner had an old car that he dragged out here and buried."

"Was there anyone in it?" Sherri asked, a reasonable question under the circumstances.

"Not that I've ever heard about," Big Larry said.

I was not completely reassured by his statement. Was there a body down there he hadn't heard about, sitting behind the wheel of some old junker? My ruminations were cut short when Sherri's cell phone rang. It was Laura. She and her husband were only a few miles away, so we exited the barn and made our way back to the house.

As we walked through the wet grass, I reviewed the evening as it had transpired thus far. What was going on at the old farmhouse? We had vague feelings of uneasiness in one room, the possibility of some bodies buried in the yard, a car buried in the barn, Little Larry's ghost stories and, oh yes, Friday the thirteenth. I didn t know what to make of all that. Nothing added up.

Headlights approached the house. Laura and her husband had arrived. After greeting each of us, Laura went upstairs. Sherri and I followed her. In the front bedroom, approximately where I had dowsed an area of energy, Laura said that she felt something as well, although not as strong as it had been when she first came out to the house a few weeks before with Sherri. That was when she had sensed the two children in the room and sent them on their way to wherever it is that ghosts go to find peace.

So, what was the presence that still lingered there? I wondered.

I would soon find out.

Despite Sherri's and my reluctance in using Ouija boards, Laura had brought one with her. Many researchers do not like to use Ouija boards because, if used improperly or by the inexperienced, unwanted spirits may be accidentally contacted. In this instance we put our trust in Laura's psychic abilities to make sure we didn't get a paranormal wrong number when we dialed the great beyond.

We all crowded around the kitchen table. The room was dark, lit only by two small candles sitting on the table. Hannah and Little Larry's lady friend started us off, the board between them. A video recorder mounted on a tripod recorded the event.

To Laura's question, *Are there any spirits here?* the planchette lightly held by the two women slowly moved toward "yes" and stopped there. Laura asked for the name of the spirit guiding the planchette. It moved over to "E," paused there, then moved to "S," then "T," then wandered over the board, seemingly confused.

"Is your name Esther?" Laura asked.

Yes.

"Did you live in this house?"

Yes.

"Are you the person who Sherri's friend saw the last time he was here?"

Yes.

"When did you die?" said Laura.

1895.

Laura continued to ask Esther more questions, sometimes aided by questions from the rest of us. We took turns on the board, relieving each other when our arms got too tired. Esther's answers now were becoming confused and we couldn't make sense of some of them. At one point Laura asked, *Do you want to be released to the light?*

The previously sluggish planchette whisked over to *No.*

"Excuse me," I said, "but shouldn't we be concerned about a spirit that doesn't want to be released?"

I thought I saw Sherri nod her head in agreement.

Just then the cameraman said that he was having trouble with the camera. It wouldn't stay in focus, even though he wasn't doing anything to change the focus. That didn't sound good either, I thought.

Laura looked thoughtful. "OK, maybe one more question. Were those your children in the upstairs room?"

Laura may have touched upon a sore point with the ghost. The planchette came to a dead stop and would not move again. We had lost contact with Esther.

That concluded our evening of ghosthunting. As I rode back to Sherri's house, I thought about what had happened. Contacting Esther only added more strangeness to an evening that was already filled with seemingly random and unconnected strange events. I wondered if all ghosthunts were like this one, but finally came to the conclusion that, how could they be any different? We were seeking logical explanations for what defied logic, logical connections for what could not be connected logically. Rationally. Further, we were getting only a glimpse of the bits and pieces of the house's two-hundred-years-plus history. Of course, they would make no sense to us.

Ghosthunting does not employ a scientific method, despite the technology used by many ghosthunters, our team included. It is more a method that relies upon the randomness of the universe, a good amount of dumb luck, and faith. The latter may be the most important.

NOTE: At the request of Big Larry, I have omitted the precise location of the farmhouse to protect his privacy.

Spotlight On:
Haunted Heartland Tours

For over seven years, Sherri Brake's Haunted Heartland Tours has taken intrepid explorers to some of the most haunted locations in Ohio and beyond. Sherri has earned a reputation as one of Ohio's most capable paranormal investigators, due not only to her investigative techniques but also to her thorough research into the history of the sites she visits.

Sherri recently moved to West Virginia and now offers ghost tours in both states. Some of her Ohio tours include the Massillon Cemetery; Five Oaks Mansion, also in Massillon; ghost walks in Canal Fulton; and the "Death by Dessert" tour of the Ohio State Reformatory in Mansfield (Sherri is also the author of *The Haunted History of the Ohio State Reformatory*, the definitive work about this intriguing location).

Sherri says her goal is to "provide quality events which blend history and hauntings. We strive to educate, enlighten, and entertain with our own unique blend of the paranormal, science, history, and local legend. Many of our events allow us to donate back to the local historical society or cemetery association involved.

"We find the best locations possible to explore history, hauntings and the paranormal. When we visit haunted locations such as the Mansfield Reformatory we secure the entire building for our event."

For more information or to book a tour, see **hauntedhistory .net.** You can also contact Haunted Heartland Tours at:

10 Scenic Highway, Summersville, WV 26651

(304) 883-2392

CHAPTER 26

Briggs-Lawrence County Public Library

IRONTON

A FEW YEARS AGO I had the pleasure of presenting a talk about Ohio ghosts and hauntings at the Briggs-Lawrence County Public Library in Ironton. Librarian Lori Shafer welcomed me to the small but modern library. The room filled to capacity, and the audience was as eager to tell me their ghost stories as I was to tell them mine, a phenomenon I experience regularly as I give presentations throughout the country; it seems that every-body has a ghost story of their own to relate.

When the talk was over and I was signing copies of my books, Scott and Amy Morgan from Southern Ohio Paranormal Enthu-siasts (S.O.P.E.), a local ghosthunting group, spoke with me and told me that the library was haunted. The library was not some old, musty building—and I didn't have any bad "vibes" about the place—but I knew enough not to judge a book by its cover, so to speak. Ghosts may attach themselves to a certain building, yes, but they may just as easily attach themselves to a particular location. It may be that in some past time that location was the site of a structure—or an event—of significance to the ghost and so it remains there, oblivious to the fact it is now haunting the newest Starbucks store instead of some pioneer log cabin or an old stage-coach inn. According to the Ironton ghosthunters, that was the nature of the haunting at the library.

Dr. Joseph Lowry was a successful and affluent physician who lived in a palatial home at 321 South Fourth Street, the location at which the library now stands. On May 24, 1933, Dr. Lowry, age 68, was found dead in his home. Dr. Lowry lived alone and after several of the good doctor's patients were unable to contact him, a friend of the doctor called on him. The door was locked and no one answered so the man climbed into the house through an unlocked window and discovered the body. The corpse had a towel placed over its face, and blood ran from the nose and mouth down the side of the face.

"That seems odd," I said. "Was the doctor murdered?"

Lori had joined us after seeing the last of the audience members out the door. "No one really knows for sure," she said.

The authorities decided that a stroke had killed Dr. Lowry and he was buried in Woodland Cemetery beside his parents. But when the key to a lock box was discovered, while the box itself remained missing, suspicions were raised that perhaps relatives that had hoped to inherit his wealth might have had something to do with his death.

Thinking that perhaps they had initially missed some bit of forensic evidence, the authorities dug up poor old Doc Lowry to have one more look at the body. They were shocked to discover that the doctor's entrails had been completely removed and that both his legs were broken.

"The entrails being removed might be explained by an autopsy, if there had been one," I said, "but the broken legs? I don't get it."

"They were broken in order to fit the body into the casket," Scott said.

"What?"

Scott explained to me that several years before his own death, the doctor had ordered an expensive casket made for his wife, who was a rather short woman. For whatever reason, the doctor reneged on his order and the undertaker was stuck with a casket too small to fit the average adult. Apparently, the undertaker had the last laugh. He admitted to investigators that when he was entrusted with the doctor's body, he broke the legs and jammed the corpse into the too-small casket. A mean act, yes, but not murderous.

To this day, no one knows for sure whether Dr. Lowry died of natural causes or whether he had a little help from some nefarious relatives. We will probably never know.

"Quite a grisly story," I said, "but what's the ghost story?"

Dr. Lowry's ghost story is typical of many ghost stories—the ghost is searching for something, in this case, his missing body parts. I'm not certain, however, how the ghost plans on repairing its broken legs, no doubt reduced to dust by now.

"So, what goes on here?" I said.

"Mostly we hear things," Lori said. "Sometimes at closing we hear the sound of jingling keys, as though someone was going around locking the doors. Even if we all hold our own keys quietly we will hear that sound."

But, I thought, the doctor wasn't a librarian. Why would his ghost be trying to lock the library doors? Did it still think it was locking the doors of its house? Or, was there another ghost in the library that had no connection to Dr. Lowry? Perhaps a former librarian, or a favorite patron of the library was still browsing the shelves.

"We've also seen the door to the Genealogy Room open and close all by itself," Lori said.

One of the weirdest stories from the library concerns a skeptical library worker who had just made her skepticism quite clear—"nonsense" was what she had said about the ghost. Just then, the computer behind her beeped. She turned and saw that the screen was now displaying a partial list of library patrons, a list she had not requested. Four names appeared on the screen, each of them with the surname "Lowry."

A moment later the computer beeped again, this time indicating that a book had been checked out. And the title? *The Ghost and Mrs. Muir.*

Ohio Haunted Road Trip Travel Guide

AMERICA'S
HAUNTED ROAD TRIP

Visiting Haunted Sites

I do hope that after reading about all these spooky places in the Buckeye State, you will want to visit them for yourself. I've made it easy for you by supplying some helpful travel information for each of them. This information was current when the book went to press, but you might want to check it out again before heading out.

And do let me know if you see any ghosts!

SOUTHWEST

Chateau Laroche
12025 Shore Rd., Loveland, OH 45140
(513) 683-4686
lovelandcastle.com
The castle is open every day from April through September, 11 a.m.–5 p.m. From October to March it is open only on Saturday and Sunday (weather permitting), 11 a.m–5 p.m. Admission is $3 per person.

Cincinnati Observatory
3489 Observatory Pl., Cincinnati, OH 45208
(513) 321-5186
cincinnatiobservatory.org
The Observatory hosts public viewings through its telescopes on Astronomy Thursdays and Fridays. Admission on Thursday is a suggested donation of $4 per person. On Friday it is $6 for adults, $4 for children under 18. The Observatory also hosts historical tours of the facility as well as other special events. Check the website for details.

Ross Gowdy House
125 George St., New Richmond, OH 45157
(513) 553-9770
The 1853 house in the Susanna Historic District is open the second Saturday of each month April through October.

Snow Hill Country Club
11093 SR 73, New Venna, OH 45159
(937) 987-2491
snowhillcountryclub com
Although Snow Hill is a semi-private country club, its facilities may be
  rented out and ghosthunters may register for the "Dinner and a Ghost"
  programs held in October; call for reservations and prices.

Promont House Museum
906 Main St., Milford, OH 45150-1767
(513) 248-0324
milfordhistory.net/programs/promont-house
The Victorian mansion, one-time home of Ohio Gov. John M. Pattison, is
  open Friday–Sunday, 1:30–4:30 p.m., and by appointment for groups of
  ten or more. There is a $5 donation for adults, $1 for children under 12.

NORTHWEST

Jenna's Mediterranean Restaurant
5629 N. Main St., Sylvania, OH 43560
(419) 842-9996
Jenna's is open Tuesday–Thursday, 11 a.m.–10 p.m.; Friday and Saturday
  11 a.m.–11:30 p.m. and Sunday 4–9 p.m. Come for the ghost, stay for the
  food!

Oliver House
27 Broadway, Toledo, OH 43604
(419) 241-1302
theoliverhousetcledo.com
There are several different culinary and entertainment venues at Oliver
  House, each with its own hours of operation. Here's the list:

Maumee Bay Brewing Co. and Brew Pub
The Café
Petit-Fours Patisserie
Rockwell's
South Wing
Mutz

In addition there are special arts and entertainment events held at Oliver House. Call the general number for more information on all the above.

Wood County Historical Center & Museum

13660 County Home Rd., Bowling Green, OH 43402
(419) 352-0967
woodcountyhistory.org
The 50-acre grounds of the former Wood County Infirmary are open year-round. The museum is open for self-guided tours from April through October and in December. Hours are Tuesday–Friday, 9:30 a.m.–4:30 p.m., and Saturday and Sunday 1–4 p.m. Suggested donations for self-guided tours are $4 for adults, $1 for children under 10.

Thomas Edison Birthplace

9 North Edison Dr., Milan, OH 44846
(419) 499-2135
tomedison.org
The home is open April, May, September, and October, Tuesday–Sunday 1–5 p.m.; June through August, Tuesday–Saturday 10 a.m.–5 p.m. and Sunday 1–5 p.m.; and November, December, February, and March Wednesday–Sunday 1–4 p.m. The last tours for all openings begin one half-hour before closing.

CENTRAL

Kelton House

586 East Town St., Columbus, OH 43215-4888
(614) 464-2022
keltonhouse.com
Kelton House is open Sundays 1–4 p.m. Admission is $6 for adults, $4 for seniors, and $2 for children 6 and over. Group tours can also be arranged. To schedule a group tour, call the Kelton House Special Events Coordinator Chuck Miller at (614) 464-2022.

Thurber House

77 Jefferson Ave., Columbus, OH 43215
(614) 464-1032

thurberhouse.org

Whether you find the ghost that scared young James Thurber or not, Thurber House is worth a visit for the literary events it hosts throughout the year, including workshops, lectures, book signings, the "Evenings with Authors" events, and its famous writer-in-residence program.

The first two floors of the house are open for tours. Call the number listed for visiting hours.

Central Ohio Fire Museum & Learning Center

260 N. Fourth St., Columbus, OH 43215

(614) 464-4099

centralohiofiremuseum.com

The old No. 16 Engine House, the last fire station built in Columbus to accommodate horse-drawn firefighting apparatus, is a favorite field-trip destination for area school children. It's open to the general public Tuesday–Saturday 10 a.m.–4 p.m. Group tours can be arranged by appointment. There is a nominal admission fee.

Ohio State Reformatory

100 Reformatory Rd., Mansfield, OH 44905

(419) 522-2644

mrps.org

There are many ways to sample the ghostly delights of the Ohio State Reformatory. The Mansfield Reformatory Preservation Society offers a variety of educational and historical tours, as well as self-guided tours, and large ghosthunting groups can rent out the facility for overnight investigations. It's a good idea to consult the website for tour schedules throughout the year and to make reservations.

Malabar Farm

4050 Bromfield Rd., Lucas, OH 44843

(419) 892-2784

malabarfarm.org

As a state park, Malabar Farm is open year-round. From May through October wagon tours of the farm are offered. Educational tours of the farm's vegetable gardens are conducted during the growing season. The Bromfield home is open all year; there is a nominal fee for the ranger-guided tour.

NORTHEAST

Franklin Castle
4308 Franklin Blvd., Cleveland, OH 44113
As this book was going to press the future of Franklin Castle remained
uncertain. The City of Cleveland condemned the building in 2010. There
are those who would like to save the historic old mansion and there are
those who would rather see a vacant lot at that location. Drive by sometime and find out who won.

Cuyahoga County Archives Building
2905 Franklin Blvd. NW, Cleveland, OH 44113
(216) 443-7250
centralservices.cuyahogacounty.us/en-US/Archives.aspx
The archives are open on Monday and Wednesday–Friday, 8:30
a.m.–3:00 p.m. They are closed to the public on Tuesday.

Local Heroes Bar & Grill
2217 E. Ninth St., Cleveland, OH 44115
(216) 566-8100
localheroesgrill.com
Located directly across the street from the Cleveland Indians' baseball stadium, Local Heroes is a great place for a post-game brew and sandwich,
but you might be sharing them with a ghost. Local Heroes is open Monday through Thursday, 11:30 a.m.–8:30 p.m., and Friday–Saturday 11:30
a.m.–9:30 p.m. On Sunday, the restaurant is open 11:30 a.m.–8:00 p.m.

Agora Theater
5000 Euclid Ave. #101, Cleveland, OH 44103
(216) 881-2221
clevelandagora.com
Visit the haunted theater's website for performances schedule. The theater
is also a regular stop on Psychic Sonya's Haunted Cleveland tours.

Lawnfield
James A. Garfield National Historic Site
8095 Mentor Ave., Mentor, OH 44060

(440) 255-8722
nps.gov/jaga
Lawnfield is open from May 1 through October 31, Monday–Saturday 10 a.m.–5 p.m., and on Sunday noon–5 p.m. From November 1 through April 30, the home is open on Saturday and Sunday only from noon–5 p.m. During those months, however, the park rangers will do their best to accommodate tour groups; call the number above to arrange a tour. Admission to Lawnfield is $5 per person over 10 years old.

Punderson Manor
Punderson State Park
P.O. Box 338
11755 Kinsman Rd., Newbury, OH 44065
(440) 564-2279 (park office)
(440) 564-9144 (manor house office)
pundersonmanorstateparklodge.com
Punderson Manor is open year-round. Call the number listed for reservations.

Stone Garden Farm & Museum
2892 Southern Rd., Richfield, OH 44286
(843) 469-4060
directory.ic.org/22851/Stone_Garden_Farm
Owner Jim Fry is a genial and accommodating host. You can drop by the farm any time, but it might be a good idea to call ahead if you want to meet Jim. Alternatively, you can visit the farm on the fourth Sunday of each month when Jim holds his dowser meetings.

The Ridges (Lin Hall)
Ohio University
East Circle Dr., Athens, OH 45701
(740) 593-1305
The Ridges (Lin Hall) is, for the most part, off-limits to would-be ghosthunters. You can get a sense of the building, however, by visiting the fine Kennedy Museum of Art located on the ground floor. Who knows if maybe the ghosts haven't moved downstairs? The museum is free and is open Tuesday, Wednesday, and Friday noon–5 p.m.; Thursday noon–8 p.m.; and Saturday and Sunday 1–5 p.m.

Moonville Tunnel
Located off Township Highway 18 (Wheelabout Rd.)
Vinton County, OH
The old Moonville Tunnel, located near Lake Hope in Vinton County, can
be visited anytime, but you should be careful of your footing, especially if
visiting at night.

Briggs-Lawrence County Public Library
321 S. Fourth St., Ironton, OH 45638
(740) 532-1124
briggslibrary.com
The library is open Monday–Thursday, 10 a.m.–8 p.m., and Friday and
Saturday, 10 a.m.–5 p.m.

Further Reading

Here are some more books about Ohio ghosts and hauntings that you may enjoy reading:

Brake, Sherri. *The Haunted History of the Ohio State Reformatory*. Charleston: History Press, 2010.

— *Haunted Stark County: A Ghoulish History*. Charleston: History Press, 2009.

Cassady, Jr., Charles. *Cleveland Ghosts*. Atglen: Schiffer, 2008.

Ciochetty, John B. *Ghosts of Historic Delaware, Ohio*. Charleston: History Press, 2010.

Eblin, Jennifer. *Haunted Miami Valley, Ohio*. Charleston: History Press, 2010.

Heinsen, Victoria King. *Ghosts and Legend of Lake Erie's North Coast*. Charleston: History Press, 2010.

Kachuba, John B. *Ghosthunting Ohio*. Cincinnati: Emmis Books, 2004.

— *Ghosthunters: On the Trail of Mediums, Dowsers, Spirit Seekers and Other Investigators of America's Paranormal World*. Franklin Lake: New Page Books, 2007.

Laven, Karen. *Cincinnati Ghosts*. Atglen: Schiffer, 2008.

— *Dayton Ghosts*. Atglen: Schiffer, 2009.

Morris, Michael and Jeff. *Cincinnati Haunted Handbook*. Cincinnati: Clerisy Press, 2010.

— *Haunted Cincinnati and Southwest Ohio*. Mount Pleasant: Arcadia Publishing, 2009.

Stansfield, Charles A. *Haunted Ohio: Ghosts and Strange Phenomena of the Buckeye State.* Mechanicsburg: Stackpole Books, 2008.

Sturtevant, Lynne. *Haunted Marietta: History and Mystery in Ohio's Oldest City.* Charleston: History Press, 2010.

Weber, Cathi. *Haunted Willoughby, Ohio.* Charleston: History Press, 2010.

Woodyard, Chris. *Ghost Hunter's Guide to Haunted Ohio.* Dayton: Kestrel Publications, 2000.

You might also want to take your ghosthunting further afield than Ohio. If so, the America's Haunted Road Trip series of ghost books from Clerisy Press are essential guides for your ghostly road trip. Titles in the series include:

Ghosthunting Florida by Dave Lapham

Ghosthunting Kentucky by Patti Starr

Ghosthunting Illinois by John Kachuba

Ghosthunting Maryland by Mike Varhola

Ghosthunting New Jersey by L'Aura Hladik

Ghosthunting New York City by L'Aura Hladik

Ghosthunting North Carolina by Kala Ambrose

Ghosthunting Ohio by John Kachuba

Ghosthunting Pennsylvania by Rose Mary Ellen Guiley

Ghosthunting Southern New England by Andrew Lake

Ghosthunting Texas by April Slaughter

Ghosthunting Virginia and the District of Columbia by Mike Varhola

Haunted Hoosier Trails and *More Haunted Hoosier Trails* by Wanda Willis

ABOUT THE AUTHOR

JOHN B. KACHUBA is the author of *Ghosthunting Ohio, Ghosthunting Illinois*, and *Ghosthunters: On the Trail of Mediums, Dowsers, Spirit Seekers and Other Investigators of America's Paranormal World*. He is a frequent presenter on the paranormal at conferences and on radio and television. For more information, see **JohnKachuba.com**.